Transforming higher ed
marketing with empathy

heart over hype

By Jaime Hunt

Contents

Author's Note		7
How to Use This Book		9
Preface		11
Introduction		15
Chapter 1:	What is Empathy-Driven Marketing?	19
Chapter 2:	Building an Empathy-Driven Brand	31
Chapter 3:	Recruitment with Heart, Not Hype	67
Chapter 4:	Marketing That Makes Them Stay	87
Chapter 5:	Busting Silos to Make Change	103
Chapter 6:	Facts Inform, Stories Transform	119
Chapter 7:	Responding to Crisis with Care	141
Chapter 8:	Accessibility: The Real Competitive Edge	165
Chapter 9:	Empathy-Driven Marketing Exercises	179
Chapter 10:	Creating Environments Where People Thrive	197
Chapter 11:	Finding the Leader You're Meant to Be	229
Chapter 12:	The Architecture of Innovation	247
Chapter 13:	Empathy-Driven Leadership Exercises	261
Chapter 14:	Final Thoughts	269
Acknowledgments		271
About the Author		275

Heart Over Hype: Transforming Higher Ed Marketing with Empathy

Copyright © 2025 by Jaime Hunt

All rights reserved. No part of this book may be reproduced, stored in a retrieval system, or transmitted in any form or by any means, electronic, mechanical, photocopying, recording, or otherwise, without the prior written permission of the publisher, except in the case of brief quotations embodied in critical articles and reviews.

Published by Pretty Lake Press

Cover design by Jaime Hunt and David Hunt

Ebook ISBN: 979-8-9923084-0-2

Paperback ISBN: 979-8-9923084-1-9

First Edition

This book is a work of nonfiction. While the author has made every effort to provide accurate and up-to-date information, some details may change over time. The publisher and the author disclaim responsibility for any errors or omissions or for results obtained from the use of the information contained herein.

For more information or for bulk orders, visit: HeartOverHype.com.

To my dad. I wish you were here to read this. I love you more.

Author's Note

Empathy is under siege. Everywhere we turn—on social media, in politics, in boardrooms, in everyday life—we see it. Empathy seems to be disappearing as our news feeds fill with stories of callousness and human suffering.

The message is clear: power is about domination and empathy is a weakness to be mocked.

We are being conditioned to believe that results are all that matter. That to lead, to influence, to succeed, we must detach. That caring is a liability. That people are obstacles to be managed rather than human beings to be understood.

But when we strip empathy away from our work, what are we left with? A world where policies dehumanize. Where institutions operate like machines instead of communities. Where leadership is defined by force rather than integrity.

I refuse to accept that.

And I believe you do, too.

This book is a call to action—to bring empathy back to our work. To push back against the idea that strength requires indifference. To reject the notion that people are expendable. To build organizations, teams, and messages that connect.

Because when we lead with empathy, we don't just make better marketing.

We make a better world.

Let's get to work.

- Jaime Hunt

How to Use This Book

My goal with *Heart Over Hype* was to create something you could take to your next meeting and immediately apply. This book is designed to be a toolkit for transforming your marketing.

Throughout the book, I use empathy as a shorthand for a range of interconnected ideas: being audience-centered, human-centered, caring, and compassionate. Whether crafting more effective student recruitment campaigns or building healthier team cultures, the core principle remains the same—putting people first leads to more impactful work.

The book is broken into two parts, each tackling an essential side of empathy in higher education: **empathy-driven marketing** and **empathy-driven leadership**. These two areas are deeply connected, but because each has its nuances, I've dedicated an entire section to exploring each.

What You'll Find Inside

Section 1: Empathy-Driven Marketing: This section explores strategies and practices that help you build meaningful connections with your audience. And, you'll discover how to infuse empathy into your work—making your marketing more powerful and impactful.

Section 2: Empathy-Driven Leadership: Marketing is just one piece of the puzzle. Without empathetic leadership, the work can feel hollow. This section focuses on how to lead with empathy to create more creative and innovative teams.

Chapter Structure

Each chapter in the book explores a core concept. At the end of each, you'll find specific steps you can start taking immediately. These are meant to help you put the ideas into practice on your campus, no matter where you are starting from.

End-of-Section Exercises

At the end of each section, I've included exercises to help guide you in implementing the lessons in the book. Whether you're working solo or with a team, these exercises will serve as a roadmap for embedding empathy (and all that it encompasses: audience-centeredness, human-centeredness, care, and compassion) into your marketing and leadership.

This book isn't just for reading; it's for doing. Let's get started.

Preface

You are so smart.

Tears welled in my father's eyes as he said it. I leaned over his hospital bed, clutching his hand in mine, willing myself to hold it together. He whispered it again, his voice weak but insistent.

You are so smart.

That moment—those words—are seared into my memory. It was the fall of 2019, and my father was dying. Even now, nearly six years later, writing them still feels like reopening a wound that hasn't fully healed.

His decline was swift. Diagnosed with kidney cancer in June, by September, he was in hospice. Just three months. Ninety days to go from hope to heartbreak.

At the time, I lived 2,000 miles away, serving as the vice chancellor of strategic communications and chief marketing officer at Winston-Salem State University. My career was thriving. I had ascended to the executive level, leading strategy at a university I deeply believed in. But when my father got sick, none of that mattered.

With the full support of Chancellor Elwood Robinson, I took extended leave to be by his side—to help him navigate the labyrinth of dying in America. To be present for the hardest goodbye of my life.

Those months changed me in ways I am still uncovering.

At my core, I am a driven professional—ambitious, strategic, relentless in my pursuit of excellence. I spent years developing the leadership skills required to thrive in an executive role. But what I didn't realize, until my dad got sick, was how those very same skills would shape my ability to show up for him in his final days.

When you're an executive, you learn how to navigate chaos. You master the art of maintaining composure in high-pressure situations. You become adept at reading the room, understanding what people need—sometimes before they even say it. You learn to set aside your emotions to focus on the bigger picture.

What I hadn't fully grasped was that these same skills are just as essential in navigating death. While negotiating with caregivers and providing stability for my family was important, what mattered most was something far more human: ensuring my father retained a sense of agency in a process where control is so often stripped away.

I have always believed that leadership is about service— that real leaders set aside their egos to uplift those around them. In those final months, I saw just how true that is— not just in boardrooms, but in hospital rooms. Not just in our careers, but in our most vulnerable moments.

Empathy is what made me a better daughter.

And my father saw that, too.

That's why, even as his body failed him, even as he faced the unimaginable, he looked at me with eyes filled with love and said it again.

You are so smart.

Not because of my degrees or my title. Not because of anything I had accomplished on paper.

What led him to say those words was watching me calm my mother, ease tensions with a nurse, and acknowledge the deep sense of powerlessness he felt. He wasn't referring to book smarts—he was talking about empathy. It was his way of saying: *I see you. I see what you are doing for me. I see that you see me. I see the woman you have become, and I am proud.*

I will carry those words with me for the rest of my life.

And I carry the lessons of those months into everything I do.

That experience reshaped how I think about leadership, communication, and human connection. It deepened my belief that the most essential skill—whether in marketing, leadership, or life—is empathy.

Empathy is what allows us to lead with heart. It's what helps us manage teams effectively, navigate crises with grace, and build brands that connect on a human level. It's what turns messaging into meaning.

When I write about empathy in marketing and leadership, it's because I have lived the difference it makes. I have seen firsthand how understanding and compassion transform moments of uncertainty into moments of clarity. How listening—not just to words, but to fears, hopes, and unspoken needs—creates trust.

Empathy is what made me a better daughter in my father's final days. It's also what makes me a better leader, a better marketer, and a better human.

And if I am so smart, it is only because I understand this:

The most important thing we can ever do—whether for our families, our teams, or our audiences—is to make them feel seen.

This book is my way of saying: *Let's put people back at the center of everything we do. Let's trade hype for heart and really make a difference.*

In the pages that follow, I'll share insights from my journey in higher education, along with practical exercises and honest stories of both victories and stumbles. I hope this book helps you create messages that make people feel seen and valued.

Because the work we do can change lives—not by shouting the loudest, but by listening better and responding with compassion.

Welcome to *Heart Over Hype*. I am glad you are here.

Introduction

In 2015, I stepped into my first C-suite role in higher education as Winston-Salem State University's chief marketing and communications officer. WSSU is a 5,000-student historically Black university in the University of North Carolina System that is consistently recognized as one of the nation's leaders in promoting social mobility.

During my first week, Chancellor Elwood Robinson dropped by my office and gestured at a poster featuring the athletics logo. "When are you going to fix that?" he asked. You'll know why if you've seen the old WSSU ram logo (seriously, Google it). Once you see it, you can't unsee it.

But Elwood wasn't just asking for a logo overhaul. He was asking for something much bigger: a complete transformation in how the university was perceived. "I want WSSU to be the first choice for Black students in North Carolina," he told me. That became our north star.

Achieving that goal wasn't going to happen with a logo alone. It wasn't even just about marketing campaigns. It required a cultural shift—a collective effort across campus. Empathy-driven marketing was the cornerstone of our strategy. We weren't just promoting a university. We were building a community where students felt seen, supported, and valued long before they stepped on campus. For WSSU, that meant putting ourselves in the mindset of our students and their families. What barriers did they face? What fears held them back? What dreams were they chasing?

I knew my budget wouldn't support hiring a full-service agency, so I rallied my team toward building the brand in-house. Over the next year, we held focus groups, sent out surveys, and spent countless hours *listening*. We also made a great effort to understand the student journey. I created a cross-functional team comprised of every student-facing department—admissions, financial aid, housing, advising, athletics, and even dining services—to map out the entire student journey.

My team and I dug deep into every touchpoint. How were students experiencing WSSU at every turn? What messages were they receiving? What feelings were we leaving them with? Were we making them feel like they belonged or like just another number? Did every message— even those about being late on paying a tuition bill—reflect the caring community we claimed to be?

We quickly realized there were gaps. Some messages conflicted, some didn't reflect the vibrancy of WSSU, and others didn't reach students at the moments they needed them most. Communications were inconsistent—some warm and inviting, others transactional and cold. And we weren't always addressing prospective students' biggest questions: "Do I belong here?" "Will I be supported?" "Will this help me achieve my dreams?"

So, we reworked everything. Emails were rewritten to reflect the warmth and pride of the WSSU brand. Orientation sessions were revamped to deliver information and instill a sense of purpose and belonging. We embedded our brand values into new employee orientations and campus-wide training, ensuring everyone—from faculty to student workers—understood and could articulate the WSSU story. And, more importantly, understood their role in telling it.

But you can't just fix touchpoints and train ambassadors. You have to listen and respond to criticisms and concerns as well. Throughout the rebranding process, we used surveys, focus groups, and casual conversations to uncover the "why nots" that discouraged students from enthusiastically choosing WSSU. There were misconceptions about outdated facilities that had long been updated, concerns about whether employers valued degrees from the university, and issues about the perceived lack of visibility in a state with eleven HBCUs. All of these insights informed our strategy.

Hearing the concerns was, at times, difficult. School leaders often want to close their eyes regarding the ugly truth. More than one has told me to ignore data points that don't paint a rosy picture of public perception. Seriously. But putting your head in the sand doesn't change reality. Data are data.

Understanding what people *really* think about who you are and what you offer gives you a chance to tell a different story. If people believe your facilities are outdated, showcase the modern new buildings on campus. If there is a perception that students don't get well-paying jobs after graduation, highlight the real facts and figures and tell the stories of your successful alumni.

Our insights told us some prospective students and their families felt the university didn't have strong academics, wasn't preparing students for good jobs or graduate school, and that campus life was boring. We threw ourselves into sharing a new narrative. We featured students who had papers they authored published in scientific journals. We boasted that our graduates had the highest salaries one year after graduation among all University of North Carolina schools (yes, even UNC Chapel Hill). Through photos and videos, we demonstrated the vibrancy of campus life.

The results were nothing short of transformational. Annually, schools across the country participate in the CIRP Freshman Survey. Among the questions asked are "Was this school your first, second, third, or lower choice? By 2018, 62 percent of first-year students said WSSU was their first choice, a leap from 43 percent four years earlier. Positive perceptions of academic reputation (66 percent to 79 percent), career preparation (54 percent to 64 percent), and campus life (60 percent to 76 percent) soared. Students weren't just choosing WSSU—they were excited about it. They *wanted* to be Rams.

This wasn't just a branding win. It was a community win. Every department on campus had a hand in this transformation. Everyone played a role, from admissions leaders who focused on customer service and made processes more straightforward, to housing staff who created a more welcoming environment for residential students to faculty who lived the WSSU mission of caring and support. It showed that branding isn't the responsibility of the marketing office alone. It's a campus-wide effort.

The power of empathy-driven marketing goes beyond filling seats or hitting enrollment numbers. It transforms how people feel about your institution and how they feel about themselves when they're part of it. When we applied this at WSSU, we didn't tell a generic tale. We built a brand —and a story—based on empathy by putting heart over hype.

Chapter 1
What is Empathy-Driven Marketing?

One of the most famous quotes in marketing comes from Harvard Business School professor Theodore Levitt: "People don't want to buy a quarter-inch drill. They want a quarter-inch hole!"

But as Seth Godin argues in his book "This is Marketing," the customer doesn't just want the outcome—a hole. With this book, I am asking you to take this saying further.

That hole will be part of something they are creating, like a crib for their first grandchild.

If we go even deeper, we know this is about more than building a piece of furniture.

What they *really* want is the moment their daughter walks into the room, sees the crib, and tears up. They want to feel that rush of connection and love when she realizes it was built, piece by piece, with her and her baby in mind.

Empathy-driven marketing challenges us to think beyond outcomes. It's not about what people want to accomplish; it's about how they want to *feel* while doing it and after it's done.

So, yes, they want the hole. And yes, they want to build the crib. But that crib will hold more than just a baby—it will hold memories. Rocking late at night when the house is still. Watching that baby take their first wobbly steps with that crib in the background. Passing it down years later, telling the story of how it was built with love.

But even that's not the whole story.

Now, let's flip the lens to the person doing the building. They want to prove something to themselves. Maybe they've never tackled a project like this before. Perhaps they've spent hours researching how to build a crib. They want to feel that resourcefulness. Every turn of the screwdriver and every dab of glue becomes part of their own story—a story of intention and effort. They want the pride they'll feel when they stand back and see their work, knowing it's the start of a family heirloom that will be cherished for generations.

And finally, let's think about the moment that makes it all worth it. They want their daughter to *feel* the love and thoughtfulness poured into every corner. They want to see her eyes light up, her hand tracing the smooth wood, and her smile when she realizes, "This was made just for me and my baby." They want that shared moment of connection that says, "I love you, and I'm here for you."

This is what empathy-driven marketing is about. Not the drill. Not even the hole. It's about understanding the emotions your product supports. It's about seeing the bigger story and showing people how your offer fits it.

Sales focuses on the drill: what it is, how it works and why it's better than others.

Marketing focuses on the hole: the outcome, the problem solved, and the value delivered.

Empathy-driven marketing focuses on the emotions: the pride, connection, and joy of creating something meaningful.

People don't just buy things. They buy *what those things make possible*. They buy how those things make them feel. Empathy-driven marketing taps into those deeper emotions. It creates connections that go beyond features or functionality. It's not about selling a product; it's about showing people how you can help them create their future, achieve a dream, or feel something they'll remember forever.

Choosing a college is no different. Students aren't just looking for a campus with pretty buildings or a list of majors—they're searching for something deeper.

Maybe they're the first in their family to go to college, carrying the hopes of everyone who's ever believed in them. Maybe they've spent hours scrolling through websites, visiting campuses, and imagining themselves in residence hall rooms and lecture halls. They are looking for a place where they can discover who they are and who they're meant to be.

They want to hear the excitement in their parents' voices and see the pride in their siblings' eyes when they share the news, "I got in!" They want to feel the weight of possibility settling on their shoulders. They want the moment their child looks up at them, proud that their mom finally got the degree she always wanted. They want the celebratory dinner after they get the promotion and raise their degree enabled. They want to know they're choosing a story they'll tell for the rest of their lives.

Yes, they want the degree. And yes, they want the career opportunities that come with it. But the degree isn't just a piece of paper—it's a symbol of transformation. It represents the friendships forged over coffee-fueled all-nighters, the professors who challenged them to think bigger, and the triumph of pushing past their limits. It's the shared memories of cheering in the student section at games, finding their voice in a classroom debate, or walking across a quiet campus at sunset, dreaming about what's next.

What they really want is the moment their parents see them in their cap and gown, tears streaming down their faces, knowing that all those late-night study sessions and moments of doubt were worth it. They want to hear their families say, "We're so proud of you," and feel the overwhelming rush of love and accomplishment in that shared moment.

This is what empathy-driven marketing is all about: understanding the emotions that drive a student's decision and helping them see how your institution fits into the bigger story of their life.

Students don't just choose a college. They choose what that college makes possible. They choose the life they're building and the person they're becoming. Empathy-driven marketing taps into those deeper emotions and shows them how your institution can help them create a future they'll be proud of.

An Empathy Manifesto

Enrolling in college is one of the biggest bets a person can make. It's a gamble with time—years of their life—and money, often borrowed. Students choose this because they believe education can open doors and create opportunity.

This book is a call to action for those who stand at the front door of the higher education experience: marketers, communicators, enrollment teams, and leaders.

This is a call to see our audiences as more than just numbers toward an enrollment goal. They're people with hopes, fears, and doubts who are making one of the most significant decisions of their lives.

Empathy-driven marketing means understanding your responsibility goes beyond filling seats. If your student pool is primarily traditional students, you are asking *teenagers* to make a massive life decision that will change the trajectory of their lives—for better or worse. If you're recruiting adult learners, the stakes are equally high. They're investing their family's resources in their dreams.

This isn't about being warm and fuzzy, either. When we oversell and under-deliver, real people get hurt. Not just their bank accounts (although that's bad enough) but their dreams. Their confidence in themselves. Their futures. We need to tell our audiences the whole truth, even when someone might choose another school.

When you approach marketing with empathy, you are no longer selling degrees. You are making someone feel seen and understood in a sea of impersonal brochures and generic emails. When you start by understanding what your audience needs and values, you can create messages that resonate. You stop shouting into the void and hoping something sticks.

Think about those high school seniors who are the first in their families to even think about college. They're probably terrified. Will they fit in? Can they hack it? Are they kidding themselves?

And parents aren't just worried about how they will foot the bill. They sit up at night wondering if their kid is safe walking across campus. Will their child have the mental health resources they need? Will someone help them if there are roommate disputes or problems with a professor?

Or that adult learner trying to balance a full-time job, three kids, and now college? They need to know you understand their reality and will help them navigate their way through it.

Sending them viewbooks with staged students lounging on manicured lawns? An email filled with higher ed jargon that makes them feel like they are outsiders? A website that requires them to know the difference between departments, programs, and majors? That's not going to cut it.

They need to see themselves. Real stories. Real struggles. Real triumphs. "Hey, I was scared too. Here's how I made it. Here's where I stumbled. Here's who helped me up."

Empathy-driven marketing shows real, messy, complicated, beautiful people that they belong.

What Is Empathy, Really?

Most people think empathy is "putting yourself in someone else's shoes." It's the classic metaphor, and it works because it captures the essence of empathy—leaving your perspective behind to step into someone else's. But empathy is much more than that.

When was the last time you felt truly understood? Not just heard, but seen—like someone had stepped into your world and grasped exactly what you were feeling. That feeling? That's empathy. And it's one of our most powerful tools for building relationships.

Experts across disciplines define empathy in several ways—and they all add a little more nuance to what it really means:

- Understanding and sharing another person's feelings*. This is empathy at its simplest: seeing

---

* Study.com. (n.d.). *Types of empathy*. Study.com. Retrieved from https://study.com/academy/lesson/types-of-empathy.html

someone else's joy, pain, or frustration and feeling a flicker of that emotion within yourself. It's the difference between watching a storm from a distance and stepping out into the rain and feeling it on your skin.

- Recognizing emotions in others and responding appropriately[*]. Empathy doesn't stop at recognizing how someone feels—it asks you to react in a way that supports or acknowledges those emotions. It's the difference between noticing someone is upset and actually saying, "Hey, I see you're having a tough day. Want to talk about it?"
- Emotionally resonating with another person's experiences[†]. This takes empathy a step deeper. It's emotional connection. It's feeling a hint of their heartbreak or sharing a slice of their joy, even if their experiences differ entirely from yours.

There are further layers of empathy. Cognitive empathy allows you to understand someone else's perspective even if you don't feel the same way[‡]. With emotional empathy, you

---

[*] *BetterHelp. (n.d.). Understanding empathy: Definition, psychology, practice, and application. BetterHelp. Retrieved December 4, 2024, from https://www.betterhelp.com/advice/general/understanding-empathy-definition-psychology-practice-and-application*

[†] *Decety, J., & Cowell, J. M. (2017). Interdisciplinary approaches to understanding empathy, prosociality, and morality. Frontiers in Psychology, 8, 1053. https://doi.org/10.3389/fpsyg.2017.01053*

[‡] *Greater Good Science Center. (n.d.). Empathy. Greater Good Science Center, University of California, Berkeley. Retrieved from https://greatergood.berkeley.edu/topic/empathy/definition*

actually feel what someone else is feeling—like their emotions are echoing inside you.

And finally, there is a next-level empathy concept called *phenomenological empathy*. This kind of empathy is foundational to the work we'll do in the rest of the book.

Phenomenological Empathy at Work

Edmund Husserl, the father of phenomenology, introduced the idea of intersubjectivity—the idea that we recognize others have their own unique experiences and perspectives. In marketing, this means observing what your audience does and understanding the deeper context of their actions.

Phenomenological empathy jumped out at me because it is rooted in concepts that resonate with me as a marketer and as a leader: unlike the basic "I feel you" kind of empathy, phenomenological empathy involves immersing yourself in someone else's experience as a living, breathing, whole person with an inner world as complex as your own. We're going to be doing a lot of that in this book.

Think about a first-generation college student exploring your university's website. On the surface, they might seem like they're just comparing tuition or checking out majors. But their reality is much more layered.

In one of my focus groups at WSSU, many of the participants spoke about feeling a mix of hope and anxiety when they were choosing a college. They were excited to be considering the next step in life, but that enthusiasm was tempered with worries. They wondered if they would fit in and if they had the chops to handle the academic work. They looked at campus photos and tried to image themselves in the scenes. What would it be like to walk through the quad, study in the library, or hang out in the student center? What would they do if it turned out their parents came up short when it came to financing their education? Who would they turn to if they had questions?

How do you reach them in this emotional moment? By speaking to their inner world. Instead of simply sharing facts, imagine saying: "We understand what it's like to be the first. That's why we're here to support you with resources and a community that's rooting for you." Pair this with stories of other first-generation students who've found success, and suddenly, you're telling a story that connects.

In her work on empathy and phenomenology, Edith Stein expanded on empathy as a unique act of consciousness—seeing someone's reality through their eyes without losing your own perspective. For marketers, this means crafting messages and experiences that reflect the nuanced reality of your audience's lives.

For example, consider an adult learner deciding whether to return to college. They're worried about choosing the right program and calculating how to juggle work, parenting, and school. Through Stein's lens, you would move beyond generic reassurance to deeply acknowledge their lived experience.

Instead of simply saying, "Flexible class schedules available," show empathy by saying: "We know balancing school with work and family is challenging. That's why we offer evening and online classes designed to fit your life, not disrupt it."

Pair this with a testimonial video of a parent who successfully navigated similar challenges, emphasizing the institution's understanding of and support for their reality.

When you design an admissions campaign, don't just see "a prospective student's stress." See how that stress feels to them in real time—how it shapes their decisions about cost, commute, and balancing family responsibilities. Address their unspoken fears with reassurance: "You're not alone on this journey, and we're here to help."

By grounding these philosophical insights in tangible actions, your marketing can move beyond transactional appeals and forge deeper, more authentic connections with your audience.

As we dive deeper into this book, we'll explore how empathy can up your marketing game and help you better connect with your audiences in ways that actually move the needle—and set you apart.

♥

Insights and Impact Plan

Hype-Free Insights

- **Marketing is About Experiences, Not Products:** Go beyond selling what you offer and show how your university or program fits into the broader, meaningful stories of your audience's lives.
- **Empathy Drives Deeper Connections:** Empathy-driven marketing focuses on understanding the emotional needs of your audience, going beyond surface-level outcomes.
- **Truth Builds Trust:** Honest and transparent marketing fosters trust and aligns expectations with reality.
- **Empathy is Multidimensional:** Effective empathy combines emotional connection and cognitive understanding, allowing you to both

feel and intellectually grasp your audience's experiences.

Impact Plan

- **Train Staff on Empathy-Driven Communication:** Offer workshops for your team and for staff across departments to ensure every touchpoint—from admissions to dining services—reflects an empathy-driven approach.
- **Audit Your Messaging Through an Empathy Lens:** If your communications seem to miss the mark, whether you are struggling to capture attention or leaving your audience unmoved, it might be time to pause and reassess. Conducting an empathy audit can reveal hidden gaps and fine-tune your tone. (See Chapter 9 for more details on how to do this.)
- **Engage in Empathy Mapping:** Develop empathy maps for your primary audiences to identify their emotional drivers. Use these insights to shape your campaigns. (See Chapter 9 for more details on how to do this.)

Chapter 2
Building an Empathy-Driven Brand

Before I start this chapter, let's get one thing straight: your brand is **not** your logo. And it's not your tagline, either. Of course, those things matter, but a brand is so much bigger than that. It's how people feel when they think about you. It's the story they tell themselves about who you are and what you stand for.

Think about your favorite brand (maybe it's Apple, Patagonia, or Starbucks). Is it the logo that makes you loyal? No. That would be silly. (Unless the logo of your favorite brand is a turtle. In that case, you're super cool and we should be friends). It's what those symbols represent. It's how those brands make you feel and what they allow you to accomplish. A logo is a reminder, not the reason.

A brand isn't what you say—it's what people feel when they interact with you. It's the story they tell themselves about who you are. And that story isn't something you can reduce to a piece of graphic design.

A brand lives in moments. The barista knows your name and order before you even ask (hi, Trae!). It's the way your laptop just works when you open it up. It's how that pair of sneakers makes you feel like you could conquer anything (New Balance 327 has my heart). A great logo might spark recognition, but these experiences create loyalty.

When people say they "love" a brand, they're not talking about its colors, font, or tagline. No, they are talking about how their favorite brand makes them feel and how the brand's values align with theirs. They love how the brand fits into their life and helps them be, or appear to be, the person they want to be.

So, yes, invest in a great logo. But don't stop there. Build a brand that means something and makes people feel something they won't forget. A logo can catch someone's eye, but a brand keeps them coming back.

Stand Out

No school in this country wouldn't describe itself as providing "a high-quality education taught by dedicated faculty in an inspiring environment."

But those are just features. And they are features of almost every college, including your competition. When everyone is saying the same thing, everyone is saying nothing. (Spoiler: there's opportunity there.) While these things matter, they don't tap into the deeply personal and emotional journey students and families experience when choosing a school.

Perhaps 20 years ago, that didn't matter. Today? It really does.

Today, your brand needs to say something and *mean* something. And what it says and means needs to rise above everyone else's story. If you present yourself the same way as everyone else, capturing attention and enrolling the type of students who will thrive at your institution becomes much more challenging.

It's Not About Features

While traveling, my husband and I visited a mall in another city. As we walked past a wayfinding kiosk, we noticed an advertisement for a local private university. The ad featured a young woman's face, next to the words, "Small classes. Big value." As taglines go, this was plain toast—bland, forgettable, and in desperate need of butter.

Why? Because it's not telling a story. It's not sparking emotion. It's just listing features and hoping people care enough to connect the dots on their own.

While features like small class sizes are nice, they're not why someone chooses a school. They're part of the equation but not the emotional driver. People want to know what those small classes *mean* for their experience. Will their professor know their name? Will they feel like their voice matters? Will they get personalized feedback on their work instead of generic comments? Saying "small classes" doesn't answer any of those questions. It leaves all the heavy lifting to the audience.

And "big value"? What does that even mean? It's so broad it could apply to anything—a good deal on a car, a coupon at a grocery store, or, apparently, your institution. It doesn't give any sense of what makes your school unique or worth choosing. (It also brings to mind the generic products that sit next to name brands at the drugstore.)

Does a prospective student wake up thinking, *I need a school with small classes*? Probably not. What they might be thinking is:

- *Will I feel lost in the crowd?*
- *Will my professors care about me?*
- *Will I get the support I need to succeed?*

"Small classes. Big value." doesn't address any of those questions. It's a cold statement of features that assumes people will draw their own emotional conclusions. It's transactional, not relational. It focuses on the institution's offerings rather than how those features impact the student experience.

"Small classes. Big value." isn't a story—it's a bullet point.

When building your brand, the biggest mistake you can make is starting with yourself—your features, your accolades, your stats. Of course, those things matter, but they're not where the story begins. If you want your brand to resonate and stick in people's minds, you must start somewhere else entirely. You have to start with your audience.

What do they hope for? What are they worried about? What keeps them up at night? What fuels their dreams?

Features might be what you offer, but hopes and dreams are why your audience cares. You miss the chance to build an authentic connection if you're not tapping into their emotions. Instead of focusing on what *you* want to say, focus on what *they* need to hear. Instead of asking, "How do we promote this program?" ask, "What hope or fear does this program address?"

Your audience is already feeling something when they come to you. Prospective students might feel a mix of excitement and anxiety—hopeful about their future but nervous about the unknown. Parents might feel protective (and maybe a little stressed) about finances, safety, and their child's happiness. Alumni could be nostalgic but uneasy about how much the institution has changed since they graduated.

Your job isn't to recite a list of offerings. It's to meet them where they are emotionally and show them how you can help *make their life better*. When you start with your audience's emotions, you create something tangible. You're not just another school talking about "innovative programs" or "student-centered learning." You're the school that is *solving their problem*.

Features in the Context of a Bigger Story

Features help define what makes your institution unique, but they should serve as proof points—not the main story. Your audience cares about more than what you offer; they want to know why it matters. Features should be positioned as solutions to problems the audience is trying to solve.

While emotion and connection should drive your brand, there are times when highlighting specific features is both appropriate but essential.

When They Reinforce a Key Area of Distinction

If your institution has a unique feature or attribute that directly contributes to student success or outcomes, it's worth highlighting. However, it should still be framed in terms of impact.

For example: instead of saying, "We have a $10 million research lab," say, "Working in our state-of-the-art research lab has helped students land competitive internships at NASA, Johns Hopkins, and Google."

When Addressing Specific Decision-Making Factors

Students and families care about job placement rates, tuition affordability, and faculty credentials, but they need context for why these things matter to them.

For example: Instead of saying, "90% of faculty hold terminal degrees," say, "Our faculty are industry leaders and scholars, meaning your classes will be taught by recognized experts."

When Overcoming Common Objections

Prospective students may be skeptical about certain aspects of your institution, especially in a competitive market. Features can be helpful when they proactively address concerns.

For example: if affordability is a concern, offer more than, "We offer financial aid." Say, "85% of our students receive financial aid, and graduates leave with 30% less debt than the national average."

When Providing Clarity to Complex Topics

Certain features, especially those related to academic programs, career outcomes, or student support services, need to be clearly articulated in a way that makes them relevant to the audience.

For example: instead of "We have a vast alumni network," say, "Our alumni network spans 50 states and 30 countries, with graduates mentoring current students and helping them land their first jobs."

Think of features as evidence that backs up the emotional connection you're trying to build. When used correctly, they help move your audience from interest to trust, from curiosity to action. The best approach is to embed them naturally within compelling narratives that highlight real student experiences.

It's Not About You

What if it's not about you? Or rather, not about your university or your program.

What if the story you tell about your institution isn't about the talented faculty? The dedicated staff. The state-of-the-art facilities. The red brick buildings. The vast alumni network.

What if instead of rooting your brand in facts, you rooted it in feelings?

Take a deep breath and think: what does "a high-quality education taught by dedicated faculty in an inspiring environment" make you feel? Probably not much.

To spark emotional resonance, we need to ask: what do these facts and features enable? What challenges do they help someone overcome?

We often assume that prospective students and their families innately understand why certain aspects of higher education matter. But the truth is, they don't always know why these features are significant, and it's on us to make the case.

Take, for example, having classes taught by faculty instead of teaching assistants. To us, it's obvious: students benefit from the experience and mentorship of someone who has spent years mastering their field. But a 17-year-old browsing your website needs context to understand why that matters.

Or consider a commonly touted fact like "90% of our

faculty hold terminal degrees." For insiders, that screams quality and credibility. To someone outside the academy, their first question might be, "What is a terminal degree?" What we see as a point of pride could unintentionally leave a prospective student feeling confused—or even excluded. "Should I know what that is? Maybe I'm not cut out for college?" That is the last thing we want them to think when they are considering college. And even if they understand what a terminal degree is, it's our responsibility to explain why that matters and how it benefits their education.

And being an R1 research university? It's a badge of honor to us, but to many students, it's just jargon. You have to show them how it means access to groundbreaking opportunities, better graduate school prospects, and mentorship that can shape their future.

Instead of saying, "We have a vast alumni network," tell the story of a student who found their first job through that network. Or the alumnus who leveraged the network to find an organ donor who saved his life.

Rather than highlighting "state-of-the-art facilities," share the experience of a student who discovered a new passion in an art studio that became a sanctuary for their creativity. Explain how being familiar with working in a cutting-edge lab prepared a student for working for a biotech company as they started their career.

These examples go beyond listing features; they're opportunities to tell a story that explains *why* they matter. If we don't do that, we risk our message landing as empty buzzwords instead of compelling reasons to choose our institution.

This approach also shifts the focus away from institutional features and onto the student's aspirations. It anchors the story in the student experience. The university is the enabler, not the hero. It's not about the university, it's about what the student will accomplish or experience *because* of the university.

Empathy-driven branding replaces shouting the loudest with showing your audience that you actually *get* them. Higher education is an emotional decision. Sure, it's tied up in practicality—money, majors, job prospects—but underneath all that, it's personal. A prospective student isn't just asking, *"Can I get a degree here?"* They're asking, *"Will I fit here? Will I find my people? Will I be supported when I fail? Will I become who I want to be?"*

If your brand doesn't answer those questions, someone else's will.

You're Not the Best

The U.S. has nearly 4,000 colleges. Can you name them all? Didn't think so. If even higher ed pros struggle, imagine what it's like for a 17-year-old.

In truth, students aren't comparing *every* college. They're not sitting down with a giant spreadsheet and whittling it down individually. They're looking for the *right* one. The school that feels like it fits *them*.

So, what's the best college in the United States? Harvard? Princeton? That small liberal arts school with the historic quad and the unbelievable endowment? It doesn't matter. Most students aren't searching for the "best" college in the world; they're searching for the best college *for them*.

And what's "best" is as unique and personal as they are.

For Alex, "best" might mean sustainability and affordability—a campus committed to renewable energy and a tuition price tag that won't leave them drowning in debt. For Sam, it might mean strong support for first-generation students or a mentor-driven learning environment where they'll never feel like a number. For Mia, it could be a thriving arts program with resources to bring her creative visions to life. For Jordan, "best" might be proximity to home, a supportive disability services office, and the feeling that campus life is welcoming and inclusive.

"Best" isn't a ranking or a statistic. It's how a student feels when they picture themselves on your campus. It's the relief they get knowing they can afford your tuition. It's the confidence that they'll find *their people* in your residence halls or student centers. It's the sense of pride that comes when they see their values reflected back at them—whether that's community service, sustainability, research opportunities, or a campus culture that prioritizes well-being.

Institutions need to stop shouting *about why they're the best* and start understanding *who they're best for.* You're not for everyone (and that's okay). Instead of trying to be all things to all students, focus on what truly sets you apart and connect those strengths to the people who want and need them.

If you're a small, tight-knit campus where faculty know students by name, show how that creates personal, meaningful learning experiences. If you're a major research university, highlight how your students work alongside world-class faculty to solve real-world problems. If affordability is your priority, don't just say, "We're affordable." Show families exactly what that means and how you're invested in helping students graduate without crushing debt.

When you approach your marketing with empathy, you stop playing the rankings game and start helping students *see themselves* at your institution. You connect with what matters to *them*, not just what you want to project.

Students aren't searching for a trophy. They're searching for a home. A community. A place where they'll be supported, challenged, and valued. A place where they'll belong. Is that the story your brand is telling?

The Three Elements of a Strong Brand

Authenticity, distinctiveness, and resonance are the backbone of any strong brand. A brand fades into the background without them—just another voice lost in the noise. It's forgettable. Uninspired. And worst of all, it fails to connect. Here's why these three qualities are essential:

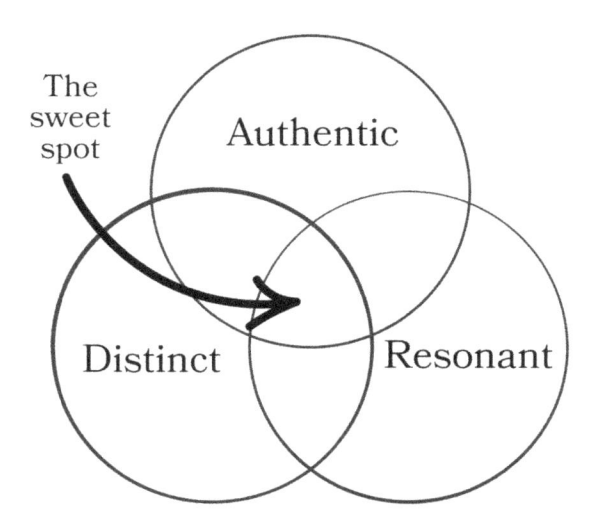

The sweet spot → Authentic / Distinct / Resonant

Authenticity: The Foundation of Trust

Let's start with authenticity. A brand that isn't authentic is like someone wearing a mask—you can tell something's off, even if you can't put your finger on it. People (especially students and families) have sharp radar for anything that feels forced, exaggerated, or fake. And in an environment where institutions are often saying the same things—"small class sizes," "world-class faculty," "commitment to student success"—what really sets you apart is how honest you are about *who you are* and *what you stand for*.

Being authentic means leaning into your strengths and owning your weaknesses. Maybe you're a small liberal arts college that can't compete with big research universities on facilities, but you can offer unmatched mentorship and community. Own that.

Distinctiveness: Standing Out in the Crowd

With four thousand colleges and universities in the United States alone, you're invisible if you're not distinct. Full stop.

Embracing what sets you apart allows you to tell your distinct story with confidence and clarity. What's unique about your campus culture? What's the one thing students can experience at your institution that they can't find anywhere else? Maybe it's a specific program, a quirky tradition, or the type of student you attract. Whatever it is, lean into it unapologetically.

Distinctiveness also means being brave enough to zig when everyone else zags. Too often, higher education brands blend into one another because they're afraid of standing out. But playing it safe is the riskiest move of all. If your message looks, sounds, or feels like everyone else's, it'll get ignored. Great brands don't say, "Pick us." They say, "Here's why we're different—and why that difference matters to you."

Resonance: Making It Personal

You can have the most authentic and unique brand in the world, but if it doesn't resonate with your audience, it won't matter. Resonance is that moment when your message doesn't just land—it *hits home*. When your audience feels like you're speaking *to them* personally. And when that happens, they don't just pay attention—they connect and remember.

Choosing a college or university isn't like deciding where to get lunch or which sneakers to buy (although I confess to spending way too much time reading reviews of sneakers). It's one of the most emotional, life-altering decisions a student will make. It's a choice filled with hope, anxiety, excitement, and a whole lot of uncertainty.

If your brand doesn't resonate, you're just another brochure in the pile, another website they skim and forget, another voice that doesn't *feel* relevant. But when your message resonates, it says, *We understand you. We see where you are. We know where you're trying to go, and we'll help you get there.* That's powerful. That's what sticks.

Listen to Your Audiences

So, how do we build an authentic, distinct, resonant brand? The first step to standing out is tuning in to your audience. They know what makes your institution unique. And if you're willing to ask, they'll tell you.

But you're not listening just to what they say. You're listening for how they feel. For the pride in an alumna's voice when she talks about her favorite professor. For the excitement a transfer student shares when they explain how they felt seen and supported during their first semester. For the words parents use when they describe the relief of knowing their child is in good hands. Those emotional insights are often the key to understanding what truly sets your institution apart.

Conduct focus groups and interview prospective students, current students, parents, alumni, faculty, and staff. Go beyond the basics and ask questions that get to the heart of their experiences:

- Why did you choose this institution?
- What's been the most meaningful part of your experience here?
- How do you describe this university to others?
- What sets this school apart?
- If you had sixty seconds to convince someone to come here, what would you say?

Then, bring in the data. Use surveys to gather both quantitative and qualitative feedback. Take a hard look at critical parts of the student journey—like application season, right after acceptance, and around graduation. This will give you a clearer picture of where your audience's needs, emotions, and expectations align (and sometimes where they don't).

And don't forget to keep an eye on what's being said about you out in the wild. Social listening tools let you analyze conversations about your institution (and competitors) on social media and forums. You'll learn what people think and how they talk about your brand—what words they use, what stories they share, and where you're nailing it or missing the mark.

What you hear might surprise you. Maybe it's not your state-of-the-art science labs or impressive rankings that get talked about most—it's the small, supportive community that made someone feel at home. Maybe alumni don't rave about their *alma mater*'s class sizes, but they can't stop talking about the mentorship they received or how much they grew during their time on campus.

These insights uncover your true differentiators.

Discover Your Institutional "Why"

The next step is to uncover your institutional "why." Not the *what*—the catalog of programs or the size of your campus. And not the *how*—the specifics of how you deliver courses or structure student support. The *why* is deeper. It's why your institution exists and the impact you're striving to make. If you can articulate that clearly and authentically, it's like a magnetic force. People don't just hear what you say; they feel it.

Start with reflection. Take a step back and dig into what your institution truly stands for. Go beyond your mission statement (honestly, many of those read like they were written by committees trying to check boxes). Ask questions that get to the heart of your purpose:

- **What problem are we solving for students and society?** Are you opening doors for first-generation students? Helping launch future innovators or artists? Serving as a lifeline for adult learners balancing jobs and families? Being a beacon for members of the military?

- **How does our approach to education transform lives?** Maybe it's through hands-on, real-world learning that leads to incredible careers. Maybe it's your commitment to affordability that ensures anyone, regardless of income, can pursue a degree. Or perhaps it's the life-changing mentorship and sense of community students find on your campus.
- **Why did we start, and what legacy are we carrying forward?** Your history matters. It's part of your story. Whether your campus is 10 years old or 200, there's a reason your institution came into existence, and that "why" can ground your messaging today.

When Simon Green Atkins founded WSSU in 1892, he was asked why he would build a school for formerly enslaved people. What would he teach them? He famously said, "What do they teach at Harvard? ... That is what I will teach here at this University." That audacious statement laid the foundation for a university built on the radical belief that education is a right, not a privilege. In a time when access to knowledge was deliberately withheld from Black Americans, Atkins refused to accept the limitations imposed by society. His vision wasn't just about creating a school—it was about dismantling barriers and proving that excellence belongs to everyone, not just the privileged few.

That spirit of audacity still drives the university. It's woven into the culture, the curriculum, and the unwavering belief that every student who walks through its doors is capable of achieving greatness. Atkins' words weren't just about the past—they were a challenge to the future. And that was a story students were inspired by.

You won't find your "why" sitting alone in a conference room. It lives in the stories and experiences of your community and in the history and traditions of your campus. Talk to leadership, faculty, alumni, and students—the people who live and breathe your institution daily. Ask them:

- What do you believe makes this place unique?
- Why do you choose to work, study, or stay here?
- What stories stand out to you as proof of our impact?

Pay attention to patterns. When the same themes bubble up repeatedly, you're getting close. Your "why" is right there, waiting to be said.

Your institution's "why" doesn't exist in a vacuum. It connects to what your audience cares about. Empathy-driven marketers look for the sweet spot—the overlap between what your school does best and what prospective students (and their families) value most.

Let's say your institution is known for its affordability and its close-knit community. If you're talking to first-generation students, your "why" might center on making higher education accessible and ensuring they never feel alone. If you're a liberal arts school known for small class sizes and dynamic learning, your "why" might focus on creating curious, adaptable graduates ready for anything and armed with a deep network.

Your "why" should speak to your audience's hopes and aspirations. It should feel like a promise that you understand them—and that your institution exists to help them thrive.

The college decision is emotional as much as it is practical. When you communicate your "why," you invite people to see themselves as part of your story. People don't fall in love with buildings or rankings. They fall in love with a story that feels true and a purpose that feels real.

Analyze Your Competitors

Working on a brand positioning project for the research portfolio of a large public research university, I faced a familiar challenge: standing out in the shadow of a flagship university, a large and very well-known STEM-focused campus, and an elite private institution—all just down the road. After conducting focus groups with stakeholders, I felt I understood what made this university tick. But was that enough? How was it truly different from the competitors that kept drawing research dollars away?

That's where the competitor analysis came in.

The kind of competitor analysis I'm talking about looks deeper than comparing tuition costs or rankings. You need to peel back the layers to understand how they're positioning themselves and, critically, where the gaps are. What are they claiming as their strengths? How are they positioning their offerings? And where does your institution's value proposition fit—or better yet, shine?

For this university, we didn't focus on being "better" than the flagship or the elite private. We focused on being distinct. The competitor analysis helped us identify a niche. My client offered rigorous research opportunities that focused on community-engaged research designed to boost an economically disadvantaged region. It combined research prestige with an emphasis on serving the greater good. That sweet spot—the overlap of rigor and service—was something none of its competitors were claiming.

The process required brutal honesty: what are we doing that others do better? But it also sparked pride: what do we do that no one else can? That clarity became the foundation for the university's positioning, setting them apart not by trying to outshine the competition but by owning their unique value.

A good competitor analysis helps you carve out your space in a crowded market. With that, you can give your audience a reason to choose you—not because the others are bad, but because you're uniquely, undeniably right for them.

What Are Your Competitors Missing?

You can't just look at what your competitors are *doing* to stand out. You have to look at what they're *missing*. You aren't scouring brochures or websites looking for flaws or mistakes. You're looking for gaps in story and finding spaces where your university can go deeper.

Start by analyzing how other institutions talk about themselves. What stories are they telling? What emotions are they trying to tap into? What student needs or concerns are they *not* addressing? How can your story fill that gap?

Another area to examine is how your competitors frame their positioning and whether they connect the dots for the audience or just list features and facts.

Let's say every school in your competitive set boasts about having "a strong sense of community." It sounds nice, but what does that actually mean? Is "community" just a buzzword they're throwing around, or is it backed up with real examples? (Spoiler alert: in most cases, it's just a buzzword.)

At WSSU, community meant having each other's backs,

no matter what. Walking across campus, students could count on seeing someone they knew. Relationships started in the classroom, but they extended far beyond graduation. I can't tell you how many times I heard alumni share that their professors—mentors who challenged them and believed in them—were guests at their weddings years later.

And it wasn't just the faculty. You could walk into a vice chancellor's office without an appointment and find someone ready to listen and help. No barriers, no gate-keeping—just a genuine desire to support students and colleagues. That level of accessibility and care defined the sense of community. For example, we often described the difference between North Carolina A&T's Homecoming and WSSU's Homecoming as "The difference between a big party and a family reunion."

These specifics matter. They make the concept of "community" feel authentic instead of generic. If your competitors paint in broad strokes, you can add detail and emotional resonance.

Next, look at how your competitors position their offerings. Are they overly transactional? Do they focus too much on rankings, job outcomes, or "value" without addressing why those matters? If they aren't—you can.

You need to compete by being *different*—and by being more human. Looking at competitors through an empathy lens helps you see where you can offer something they can't (or haven't thought to). This lens helps you pinpoint what makes your institution unique and uniquely valuable to the people you're trying to reach.

At WSSU, we didn't tout that we were the "best" in every category. We touted that we were the best place for a student who wanted to be part of a close-knit group of people who would become like family. We boasted about being a place filled with people who desired to serve their communities after graduation. We bragged about the extraordinary efforts faculty, staff, and donors made to ensure that every student had a chance to graduate—even if they fell on hard financial times. And we emphasized that our students were part of a legacy that stretched back to that bold founder, Simon Green Atkins.

These types of emotional differentiators are gold. They're the reasons students choose *your* institution over another.

Your Competitors Outside Higher Ed

When you think about competition in higher ed, it's easy to focus on other colleges and universities. And yes, those institutions are part of the equation. But they aren't the *whole* story. Students aren't just comparing your institution to another campus. They're weighing you against a range of options and influences in their lives.

Not everyone chooses college. Some prospective students are debating whether to go to school at all. For them, it's not *your* university vs. another one—it's your institution vs. the workforce, a gap year, trade school, or online certification programs. Those alternatives can feel faster and cheaper. And if your messaging doesn't address that perception, you're leaving students on the fence with no reason to choose you. You have to address these common issues head-on.

- If students are worried about cost, don't just talk about tuition. Talk about the ROI of education, what life looks like after graduation, and how you help get them there.

- If they're considering alternatives like a trade school, highlight the unique value of your programs—like the interdisciplinary skills or lifelong network—they can't get anywhere else.
- If your digital presence is lagging, invest in user-friendly experiences that meet the expectations set by today's most-loved brands. (Yes, you *are* competing with Apple's website.)

Then there's the noise. You're not just competing with other colleges for attention. Prospective students are constantly bombarded with faster, slicker, and often far more engaging content than the average university email or website. If your marketing doesn't break through, you'll be ignored—not because students don't care, but because they're overwhelmed.

And we can't forget the expectations set by the outside world. Students and parents don't just measure your website against other colleges' sites; they measure it against every digital experience they encounter. Think about the effortless convenience of buying a plane ticket on Delta or streaming on Netflix. That's the standard now.

If prospective students have to wade through five links to find the application, many will lose patience and move on. If your pages are slow to load, weighed down by flashy but unnecessary carousels—or worse, if users have to wait for carousels to cycle back to the beginning to access what they need—they'll quickly lose interest and leave. And if tuition and fees are hard to locate or unclear, students will likely abandon the process altogether.

To analyze competitors outside of higher ed, start by thinking about the brands and options your prospective students interact with daily, like tech companies, lifestyle brands, or media outlets. What are they doing that grabs attention and makes people choose them?

Check out their websites and social media channels. Sign up for their mailing lists. Notice how they explain their value and make things easy to understand. Observe how they work to connect emotionally with their audience. How do they handle objections? How do they make their benefits crystal clear? Tools like a simple analysis of strengths and weaknesses or mapping out the customer journey can help you break it down. The key is to look for ideas you can adapt to higher ed.

How to Make Data Your Empathy Co-Pilot

Now, it's time to explore the data. When it comes to understanding what works and what doesn't, data is like a roadmap. It gives you the confidence that you are making informed decisions. Empathy helps you connect with your audience's feelings and experiences, but data tell you *where* to focus that empathy. You are looking for patterns and insights that show what your audience values.

But data has to be layered with empathy. Behind every "click" and every "view" is a person. When you combine data with a genuine effort to understand those people, your marketing stops being noise and becomes something that inspires and connects.

Begin by asking the right questions: what is resonating? What falls flat? Where are people visiting, and where are they dropping off our website? Data hold the answers if you're willing to look.

Here's how you can uncover the gold:

Dig Into Your Website Metrics

Look at website traffic, click-through rates, and time on page. These numbers show you what people care about. If a page about your study abroad program gets more visitors than you expected, that's a signal. The students considering your campus are drawn to global experiences. *Lean into that.*

Or maybe a blog post about financial aid is outperforming everything else on your site. That's a neon sign pointing to a topic your audience finds important. Think about ways to expand on it. Can you create a video series on demystifying the financial aid process? An FAQ page written in plain, relatable language? A social campaign that breaks down the difference between grants and loans?

Track What Content is Actually Engaging

It's one thing to get eyeballs on your content. It's another to keep them there. Look at what people share, comment, or watch to the end. Pay attention if a video about student mentorship programs consistently outperforms other videos. It's telling you something. Mentorship might be a huge differentiator that sets you apart from the sea of institutions all touting "academic excellence" and "community."

Now, look at social media. Which posts spark conversation? Which ones get ignored? Social media engagement is often the clearest window into what your audience connects with emotionally. If posts featuring student success stories get the most traction, that's a clue. Your audience craves relatable, human-centered stories that show what's possible.

Learn From Enrollment Trends

Enrollment data aren't just numbers—they are a story about what programs and promises draw students in. Dig into it. Are there specific majors or pathways that keep growing year after year? If so, why? What's the appeal? Is it career outcomes? Cutting-edge curricula? The reputation of a particular faculty member?

On the flip side, look at what's declining. Where are you losing momentum, and what might that tell you? Sometimes, data reveal an opportunity to refresh how you position specific programs or initiatives—making them more relevant to what students want today (not five years ago).

Listen to the Students Who Enrolled ... And Those Who Didn't

One of the most underused sources of insight? Feedback from students who enrolled and the ones who didn't. Ask them why they selected another school. Their answers are invaluable. If admitted students say they loved your campus tour because it felt warm and personal, that's a strength you can lean into in your storytelling. If unenrolled students mention that another school had better communication about scholarships, that's an opportunity to improve.

Facing the Truth

No institution is immune to criticism. Whether it's concerns about cost, academic rigor, campus culture, or outdated facilities, negative perceptions about your school exist—whether you acknowledge them or not. Ignoring them doesn't make them disappear; in fact, it often makes them worse.

Prospective students and their families often form opinions about your institution long before they set foot on campus. Negative perceptions can influence whether they even consider applying. If you don't know what's being said, you can't correct misinformation or address valid concerns in your marketing and outreach.

How to Address Negative Perceptions

- **Listen First:** Conduct surveys, monitor social media conversations, and pay attention to the feedback students, alumni, and prospective families are giving.
- **Actively Work on Solutions**: If a perception is rooted in reality, create an action plan for change and communicate those improvements clearly.
- **Shape the Narrative**: Proactively share positive stories that counter negative perceptions. Use storytelling to highlight stories that dispel the stereotypes about your institution.
- **Engage Key Messengers:** Your campus alumni can be your best advocates. Give them the tools and information they need to push back against misperceptions in an authentic way.

Focus on the "Feeling" of Your Brand

What *really* sets your institution apart is how it makes people *feel.* Because when someone feels something, they remember it. They connect to it. And that's where real brand loyalty begins.

Think about your prospective students. What emotions do you want your brand to spark in them? Do you want them to feel inspired and confident—like their biggest dreams are within reach? Or maybe reassured and supported—like this is a place where they'll be seen and cared for? What about excitement—that buzz that says, *"This is where I want to be. I can picture myself here."*

The answer will depend on who you are as an institution. A small liberal arts college might lean into feelings of belonging, intimacy, and personal growth. A powerhouse research university might evoke inspiration, opportunity, and a sense of limitless possibility. Your brand isn't just what you *say* you are. It's how you make your audience *feel* at every interaction.

Once you've nailed down the emotions you want to evoke, let that guide your brand's personality—how you show up in tone, visuals, and messaging. If you want students to feel supported and encouraged, your tone of voice might be warm, friendly, and approachable. Think "Let's figure this out together" instead of "We are an institution of great prestige" (cue the dry, impersonal copy). If your focus is inspiration and bold ambition, your visuals might lean into sweeping campus shots, high-energy student stories, and dynamic language that says, *"Let's change the world together."*

Every touchpoint matters—your website, emails, social media, and even the campus tour. Every interaction should reinforce that feeling. A brochure that feels cold and corporate when your brand is all about warmth? That's a disconnect. A website that's cluttered and confusing when your promise is simplicity and support? Same thing.

And don't just rely on your gut. Test it. Run messaging by your audiences and ask: *how does this make you feel?* Does it reflect the tone you're aiming for? If not, keep refining it until it clicks.

Co-Create with Your Community

The best ideas for your brand don't always come from a conference room or a leadership meeting. In fact, they rarely do. If you want your institution to feel authentic, vibrant, and genuine, you must build it with the people who know it best: your community.

Start by creating opportunities for the community to contribute. And don't overthink this. Sometimes, it's as simple as asking.

Host Workshops or Brainstorming Sessions: Invite students, faculty, alumni, and parents to share their ideas. You can make it fun and informal or more structured with facilitated focus groups. Ask questions like:

- "What makes this place feel like home to you?"
- "What's your favorite memory here?"
- "How would you describe this university to a friend?"

The answers will surprise you (and probably move you). You'll hear things you hadn't considered—moments, traditions, and experiences that resonate deeply with those who live them.

Elevate Student Voices: Students are your most potent storytellers because they live the real-time experience. Encourage them to share their perspectives, whether it's through testimonials, blog posts, or Instagram takeovers.

User-generated content gives prospective students an unfiltered look at campus life. It builds a brand that feels alive and real because it *is*.

Partner with Campus Groups: The diversity of your community is one of your biggest assets—so showcase it. Collaborate with cultural organizations, student leadership, athletics, and academic departments to ensure your brand reflects the richness of campus life. Don't just tell their stories – amplify their voices. Representation matters. And people want to see themselves in your institution's identity.

Inviting your community to co-create builds a brand rooted in *reality*, not vague, top-down messaging. The brand becomes a reflection of shared experiences, pride, and culture. You also foster a sense of ownership. When people see themselves reflected in the brand, they connect with it on a deeper level. Students become advocates. Alumni become ambassadors. Faculty and staff feel invested in the institution's story.

Authenticity can't be manufactured. But it *can* be uncovered when you bring your community into the process. Your distinctiveness—your "why"—is already there. The stories, the voices, the values just need a platform.

It's All Marketing

You might have marketing in your title.

Your office might be called University Marketing and Communications.

But you are not the only marketers.

Everything communicates *something* about your university. It's easy to think marketing is just the stuff we do in the marketing office. But marketing is everything. It's how the university makes people feel in every interaction, big or small. It's in how people experience your institution well beyond viewbooks and ads.

Even a phone call shapes your brand. A warm, helpful voice says, "You matter." A rushed tone says, "We don't have time for you." And they'll remember how that moment felt long after they've forgotten what was said. Every call, every email, every conversation—it's all part of the bigger picture.

Even the benches on campus tell a story. Yes, benches. Are they designed for connection—or are they afterthoughts? You might not think a bench can sway someone's impression of your school, but it's part of a bigger pattern. Every detail contributes to the feeling someone gets when they step onto your campus.

Everything you do either builds your brand or chips away at it. It's not just the big, obvious efforts; it's the everyday stuff, too. The way you greet people on a tour, the clarity of your website, the kindness of a professor, and even the landscaping on campus tell a story.

Marketing isn't a job for one team or department. It's a culture. A mindset. It's the thread running through every interaction, every decision, every moment. When that thread is strong and intentional, it weaves a story people won't forget.

A Shared Responsibility

Building your university's brand isn't something the marketing office can tackle solo. It's a team effort—a whole campus effort. But not everyone on campus sees it that way. Some might think, *"Marketing's got this. It's their job to handle the brand."* And sure, your team might be the experts in messaging, design, and strategy. But the brand? The brand is much bigger than that. It's every single experience someone has with your institution. And that means everyone plays a role.

So, how do you help the rest of campus see their part in the bigger picture? It starts with showing them that brand isn't just a marketing thing—it's an *everything* thing.

Share the Why Behind the Brand

First, people need to know what the brand represents. Think beyond the campaign concept or visual identity. Why does your university exist? What makes it different from the one down the road? And why should anyone care?

It's your job to ensure the message is clear and accessible and not buried in a 50-page strategy doc no one reads. Talk about the brand in ways that connect to people's day-to-day roles. Maybe you attend a department meeting and say, *"Here's how our brand fosters belonging and how your work directly impacts that."* Or share real-life examples of the brand in action, like a professor who goes the extra mile for their students or a custodian who makes visitors feel welcome with a smile and a kind word.

It's not enough to say, *"Here's our brand."* You have to make people feel it—and see themselves in it.

Show How the Little Things Add Up

A brand isn't just shaped by the big moments. Sure, the viewbook, the website, and social media posts matter. But so do the small, everyday interactions. The way someone is greeted on a campus tour. How clean the bathrooms are on move-in day. The tone of an email sent from financial aid.

These moments might seem minor (even invisible), but

they add up to something big. A prospective student might not remember every detail of a tour, but they'll remember how they *felt*. And that feeling is tied directly to your brand.

Share these insights with your campus. Help people see how their actions—no matter how small—impact how others perceive the university. Use specific examples, like, *"When you go the extra mile to help a lost visitor find their way, you're showing them what we're all about."* Or, *"When we send a clear, kind email about billing, it builds trust with families."*

Make Everyone a Brand Ambassador

Most people don't see themselves as "marketers." But they are. Everyone on campus is, whether they realize it or not. So, give them the tools to step into that role with confidence.

Offer simple, straightforward training—nothing corporate or overwhelming. Maybe it's a quick session during staff orientation on what the brand stands for and how they can embody it. Or a cheat sheet for faculty on how to answer prospective student questions during open house events.

And don't forget the leaders. Deans, directors, and senior staff set the tone for their departments. If they don't understand or buy into the brand, getting their teams on board will be hard. Spend time with them. Make sure they get it—and that they see why it matters.

Build a Culture of Collaboration

Here's a pro tip: people are way more likely to embrace the brand if they feel part of building it. So, make it a team effort.

Bring different departments together to brainstorm how they can bring the brand to life in their work. Partner with student life to make sure campus events align with your messaging. Work with admissions to ensure tours feel authentic and on-brand.

Don't just hand them a script and say, *"Here, follow this."* Ask for their ideas. Listen to their insights. When people feel included in the process, they're more invested in the outcome.

Lead by Example

It starts with you. If you want your campus to embrace the brand, you must model it. That means showing empathy, collaboration, and authenticity in your leadership. It means communicating the brand vision consistently and passionately (not just checking it off a to-do list). And it means walking the walk.

When you lead with the brand in mind, others follow. And when the whole campus understands its place in building the brand, you're making a movement.

Insights and Impact Plan

Hype-Free Insights

- **Your Brand is an Emotion, Not a Logo**: A brand is the feeling people associate with your institution, the story they tell themselves about who you are—not your logo, tagline, or offerings.

- **Empathy is the Foundation of Connection**: Build your brand by understanding and reflecting your audience's emotions. Show them their potential, not just facts.
- **Experiences Shape Perceptions:** Every interaction with your institution—from a campus tour to a financial aid email—contributes to your brand. Ensure all touchpoints align with your core values.
- **Stories Over Stats:** Facts inform, but stories transform. Highlight the emotions and aspirations behind your offerings to create deeper connections.
- **Data + Empathy = Impact:** Use data to uncover what resonates with your audience, then pair it with empathy to create messages that inspire action.

Impact Plan

- **Listen to Your Audience**: Conduct interviews or surveys with students, parents, and alumni to uncover emotional insights. Ask questions like, "What made you choose us?" or "What's been your most meaningful experience?"
- **Identify Your Differentiators:** List what makes your institution unique. Focus on specific aspects of your story that set you apart from competitors.
- **Craft an Emotional Story**: Create a short narrative that captures your institution's "why"

and the feelings you want to evoke. Test it with your audiences to see if it resonates.
- **Enhance Key Touchpoints**: Focus on moments that matter, like campus tours or application emails. Ensure they reflect the emotions the audience may be experiencing.
- **Co-Create with Your Community:** Host brainstorming sessions with students, faculty, and staff to uncover authentic stories and ideas for bringing your brand to life.

Chapter 3
Recruitment with Heart, Not Hype

A high school senior stares at his phone late at night. His inbox overflows with emails from colleges, his Instagram feed is packed with ads, and his desk is buried under viewbooks and postcards. The future looms like an enormous wave, and he's not sure he's ready to dive in.

Across town, a woman opens her laptop after a long day at work and a long night working on homework with her kids. She dreams of getting a degree and changing her family's financial situation, but she's not sure where to start. She submits an inquiry form on a college search website, and suddenly, her inbox is crammed with near-daily messages pressuring her to APPLY NOW. Her work life, kids, and family all want a piece of her. And now she feels hounded by colleges, too.

Prospective students and parents are inundated with messages from multiple institutions, each vying for attention with similar promises and calls to action. While keeping your school top of mind is important, overloading prospective students' inboxes can have the opposite effect—driving them to disengage entirely.

There has to be a better way. Colleges keep turning up the volume—more emails, more mailers, more texts—hoping something sticks. But instead of drawing students in, they're driving them away. Just like my favorite clothing stores and favorite bookstores flood my inbox daily with emails I rarely read, these nonstop, impersonal messages start to feel more like someone is checking off a box than trying to make a real connection.

This is where empathy-driven recruitment comes in. When we center our work in empathy, we slow down and think about the audience's perspective. Instead of flooding inboxes and mailboxes with generic information, we answer the questions they're *actually* asking.

And don't focus on just the prospective students themselves. Their parents and guardians also navigate a maze of questions and fears. Empathy-driven recruitment understands this. It acknowledges that every person on this journey has worries and hopes.

Timing matters. Tone matters. Volume matters. And most of all, understanding matters.

The call for empathy-driven recruitment is a call to be more intentional and thoughtful, and to see the college journey through the eyes of the people living it. When you do that, you are positioned to create messages that resonate and feel human—not robotic or forced. And when a school takes the time to listen and adapt, it can transform your institution from "a place to study" to "a place that feels like home."

Mapping the Student Journey

Students don't live in a vacuum—they balance class schedules, family pressures, financial worries, and mental health struggles. If your communication doesn't acknowledge their reality, it's going straight into the digital abyss.

For years, colleges and universities have seemingly worked under the assumption that tossing out information was enough to help students make life-changing decisions. It's not. We need to shift the focus from providing information to meeting a need. At the heart of this approach is the student journey map.

Creating a journey map starts by stepping outside your campus bubble and seeing things through your prospective students' eyes. The goal is to understand where they are in the journey from both a timeline perspective and an emotional one. Every step—from hearing about your school for the first time to stepping foot on campus—is a mix of moments, both pivotal and mundane.

A journey map helps you understand timing and relevance and gives you the tools to show up with answers just before they have the question. Moving away from transactional communications to communications with heart puts your university over the edge of competitors.

Without a journey map, communication feels robotic—just emails and sales pitches with no clear path. With a journey map, every interaction becomes an opportunity to reduce stress and build excitement. Instead of asking, "What do we need to tell them?" ask, "What do they need right now?"

The best journey maps highlight more than milestones—they uncover the headaches. A confusing application portal or a vague scholarship process might not seem like a big deal to staff, but those moments can be when doubt creeps in for students. The goal is to eliminate friction wherever it exists.

Mapping the student journey encourages collaboration

69

between departments. Students don't see silos—they see one institution. It's time we started acting like it.

When creating a map, start by asking these questions about each step of the journey:

- What is the audience *thinking*?
- What are they *doing*?
- What are they *feeling*?
- What questions are they *asking*?
- Who is *influencing them*?
- What *action* do we want them to take?
- What *barriers* prevent them from taking that action?
- How can we show we *care*?

Document the answers at each milestone and let that document guide what you say and how you say it. Are they excited about a new opportunity, overwhelmed by decisions, or maybe stressed about finances? Each phase of their journey comes with a unique cocktail of emotions. Understanding this helps you craft messages that make a deeper connection.

You will uncover moments when students don't want or need a sales pitch. They need clarity. Think about the FAQs you hear over and over at certain points of the journey and address those proactively. (And please make the answers easy to find. If they have to dig through five links, they're already halfway to closing your tab.)

And remember: tone matters. It's not just what you say but how you say it. An overwhelmed student doesn't need a generic "apply before it's too late" email. That just ratchets up anxiety. Instead, communicate with a tone that says, "Hey, we know this is hard. Let's make it easier together."

Small Gestures, Big Impact

Empathy doesn't always require sweeping gestures. Sometimes, the simplest, most thoughtful actions can have the biggest impact.

- **Use Their Name:** It sounds almost too easy. But addressing students by name in communications adds a personal touch. Instead of feeling like one of many, they feel like someone is talking to *them*. Whether it's "Hi Maria, we're excited to see your application come through!" or "Great job on completing your scholarship application, Malik!" it takes a few extra seconds but shows that you're paying attention.
- **Celebrate Milestones**: One of my favorite things is when I check off a task in Asana and see the rainbow-haired unicorn fly across the screen. Maybe it's silly, but it feels like a mini celebration of a small accomplishment. We all love a little recognition, and students are no different. When they hit a milestone—no matter how small—acknowledge it. That first completed application? It's a really big deal. Turning in a scholarship essay on time? That's worth celebrating. It could be as simple as an email saying, "Way to go!" or a short text cheering them on. These moments help students feel like their efforts matter to someone beyond themselves.
- **Write Like a Human:** Students don't respond to formal language that reads like a committee

wrote it. Drop the jargon and talk like a real person. For example, skip the academic tone if you're announcing a new resource. Instead of "The Office of Undergraduate Admissions is pleased to inform prospective students of enhanced application support services," try, "We've rolled out a new tool to make applying easier." Save the formality for formal occasions (and maybe even consider ditching it there).

- **Acknowledge Communication Overload:** Students and families are constantly bombarded by messages. By acknowledging this reality, you show you understand what they're going through. A line like, "We know you've got a lot of messages coming your way, so we'll keep this short and sweet," not only sets your communication apart but shows empathy for their experience.
- **Invite Feedback:** Empathy means listening. Add a "Was this helpful?" link to the footer of your emails. Then, track responses and tweak messaging based on student feedback.

Less Is More

Many enrollment management and marketing leaders seem to believe their university will be forgotten if they do not constantly send out messages. This fear drives many institutions to overload students with emails, print pieces, texts, and phone calls, hoping that something will stick. But bombarding students non-stop doesn't make you stand out, at least not in the ways you want.

Students are savvy. They know when a message is just

noise. And they are frustrated with irrelevant communications. Once they start ignoring your messages, it's tough to regain their attention. Worse, over-communicating can lead them to a negative perception as they associate you with spam instead of meaningful engagement.

Rather than focusing on quantity, focus on purpose. Each message you send should feel helpful and necessary. Ask yourself three key questions before hitting "send":

- **Why does this matter to them?** Students won't act on your message unless they see its relevance to their lives. Highlight what's in it for them, whether it's making their application process easier, giving their scholarship application priority, or answering a question they might have.
- **What action do I want the student to take?** Every communication should have a clear purpose. If the goal isn't immediately apparent, your message doesn't matter.
- **Is it easy for them to act?** If the next step isn't straightforward, students will likely abandon it altogether. Avoid overwhelming them with multiple calls to action or vague instructions. Instead, focus on one specific step they can take immediately.

The Cost of Clutter

Imagine a student receiving three emails from your institution in one day: one with a general "Apply Now" message, another about financial aid deadlines, and a third about an upcoming admissions event. Even if each message is valuable, the sheer volume creates fatigue. The student might ignore all three—or worse, unsubscribe entirely.

But clutter isn't just about volume; it's about timing and relevance. If your messages feel disjointed or lack a clear focus, they'll blend into the background noise of a prospective student's busy life. To avoid this, prioritize intentionality. Only send messages that align with the student's current stage in their journey.

When you focus on quality over quantity, each interaction becomes an opportunity to strengthen your relationship with the student. A thoughtfully timed, personalized email has far more impact than a dozen generic ones.

Here are some ways to add value:

- **Segment Your Audiences:** Tailor your communications to specific groups, such as admitted students, transfer students, or international applicants. A "one-size-fits-all" approach is a fast track to irrelevance.
- **Focus on Timing:** Map out a communication plan that delivers messages when they're most useful. For instance, an email about orientation details should arrive closer to the student's enrollment date, not months in advance.
- **Use Data to Inform Your Strategy:** Track which messages students open and click on. This data can help refine your approach and identify what resonates with your audience.

Clarity Above All

Clarity is a superpower. Students will actually *remember* an institution that respects their time by keeping communication simple, actionable, and—dare I say it—helpful. It's the kind of thing that makes them think, *Hey, these people get it!*

Students shouldn't feel stuck in an escape room adventure to figure out what your email asks them to do. If they must hunt for key details or decode academic jargon, guess what. They're not going to do it. And honestly, can you blame them?

Our job is to make things simple. Every message should be clear about its purpose and, more importantly, make it ridiculously easy for students to act on. Save the ten-paragraph essays for their English classes, not your email updates.

The magic of clarity is its **simplicity** and **intentionality**. Here's how to cut through the noise, stand out, and give students exactly what they need without making them roll their eyes or hit delete.

- **Eliminate Jargon and Complexity**: Higher education is rife with industry-specific terms and academic jargon. While these phrases might make sense internally, they can alienate students who are unfamiliar with them. For example, instead of referring to "co-curricular activities" try "student clubs and organizations." Similarly, lengthy explanations of processes or programs can overwhelm rather than inform. Instead, write as if you were speaking directly to the student in a conversation, or use an explainer video. Be sure to use language that is approachable and concise. Remember, your goal isn't to impress them with vocabulary; it's to communicate effectively.

- **Structure for Readability**: Even the clearest message can fail if it's buried in dense paragraphs or an intimidating wall of text. Students often skim rather than read thoroughly, so make it easy for them to find the most important points quickly. Make the key points bold and use headers to break up blocks of text.
- **Craft Strong Calls to Action (CTAs)**: Every message should have a clear purpose, and your call to action (CTA) is where you make that purpose explicit. A vague or complicated CTA leaves students guessing, often resulting in no action. Effective CTAs are:
  - **Direct**: Clearly state the next step. Instead of "Learn more about financial aid," say "Complete your financial aid application [link] by [deadline]."
  - **Singular**: Focus on one action per message. Avoid giving students multiple, competing options like "Sign up for this event, check out this guide, and contact us for more info."
  - **Actionable**: Use strong, imperative verbs like "Apply now," "Schedule a visit," or "Choose your housing."

Students feel supported and confident when your messages are clear and easy to follow. They're more likely to engage with your communications and less likely to feel overwhelmed or confused. Over time, this fosters trust and reinforces the idea that your institution values their time and success.

Conversely, unclear messages can erode trust. If

students are constantly left with questions or feel like they're missing critical details, they may doubt your institution's ability to meet their needs. Prioritizing clarity makes life easier for students, guiding them through their journey without unnecessary confusion or frustration. When your communications are seamless, students notice, and they trust you more.

The best message isn't the one that gets read; it's the one that gets *acted* on. And that is how you turn clarity into your institution's competitive edge.

Timing is Essential

We talk a lot about empathy in terms of feelings—understanding what our audience cares about and connecting emotionally. But empathy also means understanding what's happening in their lives at any moment. It's not just their feelings that matter; it's their circumstances, their priorities, and how your message fits into their busy world.

A friend once worked on an announcement that would transform her campus. This wasn't just big news; it was groundbreaking. It would reshape the university's future, open up new opportunities for students, and leave a mark on the entire region. It was the kind of announcement that should dominate headlines and spark conversations across higher ed.

But her leadership chose December 21 for the big reveal.

When she told me the story, I cringed. I knew what was coming next. "We got a tiny blurb in the local paper, and that's it," she said. And there it was—the inevitable outcome of launching major news three days before Christmas. Journalists already had their holiday stories filed, inboxes were ignored, and the audience's attention was elsewhere. The story was dead on arrival.

Timing Matters for Students, Too

This lesson doesn't just apply to media relations. It's just as important when you're communicating directly with students. I learned this firsthand during my time at WSSU. One of my hard-and-fast rules? Never make a major announcement that would impact the audience on a Friday afternoon.

Why? A few reasons. First, I didn't want to put my social media manager in the line of fire over the weekend, dealing with a flood of frustrated messages while the rest of us were offline. But more importantly, I knew that if students had questions or concerns, there would be no one around to answer them. Offices would be closed, and the people who could provide clarity or solutions would be enjoying their weekend. Frustrations would grow. Simple questions would turn into anger. And by Monday, what could have been a manageable situation would be a full-blown crisis. That's just a bad strategy.

Timing also applies to enrollment marketing. Raise your hand if your campus bases its drip campaigns around your dates and deadlines. Keep it raised if your campus also considers what's happening in a student's life when scheduling those campaigns. I'm guessing a lot of hands just dropped.

If you're recruiting traditional students, it's not enough to think about your calendar—you need to think about theirs. High school students live by a different rhythm than your campus. Ignoring that means your perfectly crafted messages might end up lost in the noise or ignored entirely.

For traditional high school students, the academic year has a natural flow. Fall? Students are settling into classes, going to football games, and, for seniors, navigating the mounting stress of application deadlines. Winter? Holiday breaks, midterms, and early admissions results. Spring? It's decision time for seniors and the chaotic buzz of spring break, prom, graduation, and finals.

If you are recruiting adult learners, think about the rhythm of their lives, too. Picture the last few weeks of August. If they have kids, they are dealing with the logistical whirlwind of "back to school" season. For many, it's all hands on deck to keep things moving. Sending an email about your program during this time? It'll likely get buried under PTA emails and reminders to pick up pencils. For adult learners, late August might be the worst moment to expect them to consider adding school to their already-packed plates.

However, think about how they feel a week or two after the winter holidays. By mid-January, the glow of the season has faded, and the reality of winter is settling in. It's cold, it's dark, and people are reevaluating their lives. New Year's resolutions are fresh on their minds—whether it's "make a career change," "go back to school," or just "do something meaningful this year." This is the prime time to put your program in front of them. A well-placed message here isn't just opportunistic; it's empathetic. It taps into their mindset. You're showing up when they're open to change and considering their next steps.

Testing: Listening Before Launching

Even when you've done your homework, assumptions can miss the mark. That's why testing is essential. It's not enough to think you've nailed the perfect message. You need to know it lands the way you intended. The only way to know that is to listen.

Start small. Share your message with a focus group of prospective students or first-years already on campus. Keep it intimate. Don't focus on presenting a polished campaign; you're looking for honest reactions. A smaller group tends to make people feel more comfortable saying, "This doesn't make sense," or "This doesn't sound like you're talking to me."

Ask for feedback directly. Simple questions work best: "Did this help? Does this answer what you needed to know?" If it didn't, find out why. Encourage them to point out what's missing or what feels off. The more specific their feedback, the better your final result will be.

Once you have that input, don't brush it aside. Adjust. If a message feels too stiff or skips over a concern, fix it. Rework it. Rewrite it. Don't waste time defending your original idea. Instead, focus on improving it. Every tweak gets you closer to a message that feels authentic and useful.

Testing isn't a one-and-done deal. Audience needs shift. What works today might not resonate six months from now. So, keep the feedback loop open. Stay in tune with the people you're talking to.

Learn and Improve Over Time

I recently chatted with a colleague who had started in a new role and was reviewing the drip campaign for first-time students.

"When I got here," she said, "I realized they've been using the same emails since before the pandemic." We just stared at each other, momentarily unsure if we should laugh or cry.

I wish I were surprised, but I honestly am not. The effort it takes to create a great drip campaign is not something anyone wishes to repeat annually. Unfortunately, we should.

The best empathetic communication isn't static. It's alive. It breathes and grows as you get to know your audience better. It's a conversation, not a script. And like any good conversation, it improves as you listen and adjust.

Start by paying attention to the numbers. Are students clicking the links to your resources? Are they responding to your posts on social media or leaving them to collect digital dust? Numbers tell a story—not the whole story, but a solid starting point. They show you where you're getting it right and where you might miss the mark.

But don't stop at the data. Pull your team together and dig into the details. Look at your messaging with fresh eyes. What worked really well? What fell flat? And why? These are opportunities to learn and improve. Maybe a certain tone struck a chord, or a message timed just right got more engagement than expected. Or perhaps something you thought was clear left people scratching their heads.

What worked yesterday might not work tomorrow. Students' lives shift. Their needs and concerns evolve. What feels urgent today—like clarity around financial aid deadlines—might fade into the background once they focus on housing assignments or course schedules. Stay curious. Pay attention to new trends, emerging concerns, and even how the world around them is changing. What matters to them should matter to you.

Every small pivot brings you closer to creating messages that resonate deeply. Empathy isn't a fixed skill; it's more like a muscle. The more you use it, the stronger it gets. And with each cycle of learning and improving, your communication becomes sharper and more impactful.

Empathy for Parents and Guardians

If you're a member of Generation X, like me, your parents' involvement in your college experience was probably minimal. Many of us were dropped off at campus with a wave and a "See you in four years."

That's not the case for today's parents and guardians. They play an enormous role in the college decision-making process as spectators, advisors, financial planners, and emotional anchors. While much of our marketing rightly focuses on students, overlooking parents is like ignoring the person picking up the tab at dinner. It's not just a bad look; it's a missed opportunity to engage a key audience.

Parents have their own concerns and hopes regarding their child's college journey. Yes, they care about tuition bills, but their involvement goes beyond finances. They're there for every stage—from narrowing down college options to celebrating graduation. They're proud of their child's achievements but grappling with the heartache of letting them go. By acknowledging these emotions and demonstrating that you value their role, you build trust and show them they matter, too.

When marketing to parents, it helps to understand the big questions they're asking. The first is practical but unavoidable: is this worth the money? College is expensive, and parents want to know their investment will pay off. This is where you highlight job placement rates and showcase alumni success stories. Tools like user-friendly cost calculators and clear financial aid guides can ease some of the stress, helping them see the value in choosing your institution.

The second question is about trust: will my child be safe and supported? Sending their child off to college is an emotional leap of faith. Parents want to know about everything from dorm safety to emergency response systems. They need to see that you have robust health and wellness services, ready to handle everything from a flu outbreak to mental health crises. Highlighting counseling options, wellness initiatives, and a strong campus community shows parents that your institution takes their child's well-being as seriously as they do.

Beyond physical and emotional safety, parents also want reassurance that their child will thrive academically and socially. What resources are in place to help students succeed in the classroom? How do you support their career goals? And just as importantly, what does campus life look like? Talk about your academic advising team, tutoring centers, and programs that help students stay on track. Share stories about residence life programs, student clubs, and events to help students build connections. Show them that your campus is more than a school—it's a place where their child can grow and belong.

Finally, there's the eternal balancing act: how can parents stay involved without overstepping? No one wants to be labeled a "helicopter parent," but many worry about how to support their child without crossing boundaries. Institutions can help by offering structured ways for parents to stay engaged—whether through newsletters, family weekends, or parent-specific portals. By providing clear channels for communication, you help reduce those frantic late-night emails about meal plans or dorm supplies.

When you take the time to engage parents thoughtfully,

you're building allies. Parents are partners in the college experience, and when they feel valued and informed, they'll become some of your institution's strongest advocates.

♥

Insights and Impact Plan

Hype-Free Insights

- **Empathy Transforms Recruitment:** Empathy-driven marketing moves beyond providing information to addressing prospective students' emotional and practical needs. It fosters a sense of belonging and humanizes the recruitment process, setting institutions apart from competitors.
- **The Power of a Student Journey Map**: A well-crafted journey map reveals both pivotal moments and potential pain points in a student's path from prospect to enrollment. By aligning communications with the student's emotional and logistical journey, institutions can build trust and reduce stress.
- **Clarity is Non-Negotiable:** Students crave simplicity and actionable messages. Clear, concise communication that is free of jargon and focused on one specific call to action builds trust and makes the institution approachable and helpful.
- **Collaboration is Key:** Empathy-driven recruitment encourages cross-departmental collaboration. Breaking down silos ensures a

unified experience for students, reflecting a cohesive and supportive institution.
- **Parents and Guardians Are Partners:** Engaging parents thoughtfully builds trust and turns them into advocates for the institution.
- **Feedback and Iteration Are Essential:** Effective communication is dynamic. Listening to student feedback, analyzing data, and iterating messages ensures relevance and impact over time, keeping the institution responsive to evolving needs.

Impact Plan

- **Audit Your Current Communications:** Review recent emails, texts, and print pieces. Eliminate redundancy, simplify messaging, and ensure each communication has a clear purpose. (See Chapter 9 for more details on how to do this.)
- **Use Empathy as Your Lens:** Before sending a message, ask: what is my audience feeling? What do they need from us right now? Adjust tone and content accordingly to match their emotional state.
- **Create Clear and Direct CTAs:** Rewrite any vague or open-ended calls to action. Ensure every message includes one clear step for your audience to take, with easy-to-follow instructions.
- **Engage Parents and Guardians:** Develop parent-focused resources like newsletters, Q&A webinars, and digital portals. Address their

specific concerns about cost, safety, and staying connected.
- **Reduce Clutter with Intentionality:** Map out a communication calendar to space messages effectively and align them with your audience's journey. Avoid sending irrelevant or poorly timed updates. (See Chapter 9 for more details on how to do this.)
- **Conduct a Timing Audit:** Evaluate the timing of messaging in your drip campaigns to ensure they fit into the lives of your audiences. (See Chapter 9 for more details on how to do this.)

Chapter 4
Marketing That Makes Them Stay

Traditionally, higher education marketing has been focused on getting students in the door. Convince them to apply, nudge them to register for classes, get them to show up. Mission accomplished, right? Not exactly. What happens after a student sets foot on campus (or logs into their first online course) matters as much as getting them there in the first place. If they don't stay and if they don't graduate, what is the point? Retention and graduation rates shouldn't be just enrollment management or academic affairs priorities. They should be marketing priorities, too.

A school's reputation isn't built on how many students it admits. It's built on how well it serves the students who enroll. This is true even of the Ivies. Yes, they get a flurry of attention for having a four percent admit rate, but if their retention and graduation rates are abysmal, they won't maintain their high rankings and reputation.

Low retention and graduation rates don't just hurt students (though that's obviously the biggest problem). They damage a university's credibility. Families notice. Future students notice. So do accreditors, donors, and employers.

If students don't finish, tough questions arise: are they struggling to find support? Does the institution care beyond orientation? Is the university admitting students who aren't prepared just to collect tuition?

Marketing is uniquely positioned to help answer those questions before they even arise.

A lot of universities have room to grow on this. They roll out the red carpet for prospective students, bombarding them with stunning marketing materials and polished videos that tout how much they'll "belong" on campus. And then? When a student enrolls, the communication shifts away from the marketing team and lands in the hands of dozens of offices across campus.

Suddenly, communications become transactional and bureaucratic. Financial aid sends jargon-filled missives that students need a translator to decode. Residence life communications are filled with language that implies that students *want* to break the rules. Five different offices send random newsletters. And the warm, welcoming energy from recruitment is gone.

This is where marketing can step in and do what it does best: make people feel like they matter. A simple, well-timed email reminding students they're not alone in struggling with midterms? That's retention marketing. A social media series featuring upperclassmen sharing their "I almost dropped out, but here's what helped" stories? That's retention marketing. Even something as small as a text message offering a nudge to check out the tutoring center or mental health resources could be the difference between a student pushing through or giving up.

If you need a business case to get involved, consider this: every student who leaves before graduating represents lost tuition revenue. If more of them stick around and graduate, it boosts the university's bottom line, strengthens the alumni network, and builds the success stories that make future students want to enroll.

So, what can marketing do to help? I have ideas.

Get Email Under Control

Colleges really love email. Need to remind students about a deadline? Send an email. Hosting an event? Email. Financial aid info, housing updates, registration reminders? Email, email, email. The problem? Students are drowning in messages, and most of them go unread. Over the last 20 years, I've held more focus groups and listening sessions with students than I can count. Not one student has ever said they receive too few emails. In fact, I've heard hundreds of students say they receive way too many.

Email fatigue is real. When students check their inboxes and see 20-plus messages from different departments, all with vague subject lines and unclear purposes, they don't stop to find what's important. They tune out. Or worse, they mass-delete everything without even opening it. The more emails an institution sends, the less effective email becomes. It's a classic case of diminishing returns.

Clean Up the Chaos

Based on my conversations with students, the biggest reason they tune out university emails isn't just the volume—it's the chaos. When multiple departments send messages independently, students end up with inboxes flooded with overlapping and redundant content. Financial aid sends one thing. Housing sends another. Career services has an announcement. The registrar chimes in. The result? Information fatigue. Students stop paying attention because they don't know what's actually important.

Instead of blasting students with multiple emails from different departments daily, universities should take a smarter approach: bundling messages into fewer, more organized emails. This doesn't mean cramming everything into a massive newsletter no one reads. It means structuring communications so students receive *fewer, more meaningful* emails that help them find what they need without feeling overwhelmed.

A well-executed weekly or bi-weekly digest can solve the email fatigue students experience. Think of it as an easy-to-read, skimmable update that highlights deadlines, opportunities, and key announcements all in one place. The trick is to structure it well. Use bolded headings, clear sections, and short, clickable summaries that link to full details if the student wants them. That way, students don't have to wade through paragraphs of information just to find out when their financial aid paperwork is due or where to sign up for tutoring.

Another way to bundle emails is through thematic grouping: sending messages that align with specific topics rather than a mix of unrelated content. Instead of separate emails from financial aid, the registrar, and academic advising, students could receive a "Stay on Track" email with registration dates, FAFSA deadlines, and academic support resources all in one. Career services, alumni relations, and internship offices could coordinate a "Future You" email that consolidates job fairs, networking events, and resume workshops. This makes information easier to process because it's presented in a way that makes sense.

Timing is also key. If universities send out a digest or bundled email at a consistent time each week, students start to anticipate it. They know they'll get an email every Monday morning or Thursday afternoon with everything they need for the week ahead. This consistency makes students more likely to engage with the content rather than ignore it.

Straighten Out Those Subject Lines

Subject lines matter. Let's say you want to let students know that the Office of Student Services is expanding its business hours to 7 p.m. Mondays through Thursdays. Don't make the subject line for that message *"Important Update from the Office of Student Services."* Why would that encourage anyone to open the message? It conveys nothing and does nothing to entice a student that the message's contents will be any better.

Instead, try something like, "Office of Student Students Now Open Until 7 p.m. Monday-Thursday." You might say, "But, Jaime, they won't open the email if I tell them everything in the subject line." Is the goal to get an open or deliver the information? (Cue awkward silence.)

And then there's the content itself. If students have to dig through five paragraphs of text to figure out what they need to do, they're already gone. Keep it short. Keep it direct. If an email is just an announcement, ask yourself—does this need to be an email? Could it be a text, a social media post, or even a push notification instead?

The goal isn't sending emails—it's ensuring students read and act on them.

Don't Skip Segmentation

Students don't have time to sort through emails that don't apply to them. When a university blasts the same generic message to every student—whether a freshman, senior, online learner or transfer—it's no surprise that most emails go unread. The solution is personalization and segmentation.

Personalization focuses on ensuring students get messages that matter to *them*. A struggling first-year needs different support than a soon-to-be graduate. A commuter student or adult learner might not care about campus housing updates. A transfer student might be frustrated getting messages about first-year orientation events that don't apply to them. When offices fail to tailor their outreach, they waste inbox space and erode trust. If students feel like most messages don't apply to them, they'll start ignoring *all* messages.

Segmentation fixes that. By breaking students into groups based on their year, major, academic standing, engagement level, or even personal circumstances (like first-generation status), you can send targeted messages that feel relevant. Instead of sending *all* students a vague "Need help? Check out tutoring!" message, segmentation allows you to reach the students who are at risk, like maybe those with lower midterm grades or students who have yet to use academic support services. Instead of blasting everyone with *"It's time to start thinking about internships!"* focus on juniors and seniors who haven't yet completed an internship credit.

Personalized, segmented communication *respects students' time* and ensures they only get the messages relevant to their experience in a way that feels intentional.

Guiding Students Through Challenges

A well-planned email or text message series can serve as a virtual guide for students, delivering key information exactly when they need it. Instead of overwhelming students with everything at once during orientation, send short, actionable messages that address common struggles throughout the semester.

For example:

- **Week 2:** How's it going so far? If classes feel more challenging than expected, you're not alone! Check out free tutoring options.
- **Week 4:** Midterms are coming up! Feeling stressed? Here's a quick list of study resources and where to find help.
- **Week 8:** Struggling to meet people? Getting involved in a club or campus event can help! Here's what's happening this week.
- **Week 12:** Registration time! Not sure what classes to take next semester? Your advisor can help—schedule a quick meeting.

These messages should be short, conversational, and student-focused—not long, formal emails that get ignored. If the university has texting capabilities, SMS outreach can be even more effective for quick reminders.

Social Media Content That Reassures Students They're Not Alone

Many first-year students look around and assume everyone else has it figured out—except them. Social media can help break that illusion by normalizing struggle and reinforcing resilience. One of the best ways to do this is through student testimonials and real-life stories.

For example:

- A TikTok or Instagram Reel featuring a sophomore or junior sharing: "My first semester was rough. I thought I was the only one struggling. Here's what helped me get through it."
- A carousel post on Instagram with the theme: "Things I Wish I Knew as a Freshman," featuring advice from juniors and seniors.
- A Twitter thread or Reddit AMA hosted by current students: "Ask me anything about surviving your first semester."
- A "Day in the Life" takeover on Instagram where a first-year student shares their real schedule, including struggles and wins.

The key here is authenticity. Use real students and unscripted content.

Quick Videos Explaining Campus Basics

Many students fear asking basic questions because they don't want to look like they don't know what they're doing. Short, friendly explainer videos can remove that anxiety by showing them exactly how things work.

Some ideas:

- **How to Drop a Class**: A 60-second video walking students through the online process,

explaining deadlines, and addressing what happens if they drop a course.
- **Where to Get Tutoring Help**: A video showing where the tutoring center is (or how to access virtual tutoring) with a student sharing their experience.
- **How to Talk to a Professor**: A video with tips on emailing professors, asking for help, and visiting office hours.
- **How to Register for Classes**: A step-by-step screen recording showing the registration system so students don't panic when their registration window opens.

These videos don't have to be high-budget productions. In fact, students often prefer informal, relatable videos over polished marketing pieces. A simple, student-recorded TikTok-style video can be just as effective (if not more so) than a professionally produced one.

Use Social Media to Normalize Help-Seeking

One of the most effective ways to raise awareness is through social media content that demystifies campus resources. Students are far more likely to engage with a short-form, relatable video than a long, text-heavy email announcing that "academic support services are available." Instead of listing resources in a generic post, universities can highlight real students sharing their experiences:

- A TikTok featuring a student saying, "I used to be scared to go to tutoring because I thought it

meant I wasn't smart enough. Turns out, half my class was going! It made such a difference."
- An Instagram Reel showing how easy it is to book a mental health counseling appointment, paired with a reassuring caption like, "Your mental health matters. Here's how to schedule a free, confidential session in less than two minutes."
- A student takeover on Instagram where a senior walks viewers through a day in their life —including stops at career services or advising —showing how normal it is to use these resources.

When students see their peers using campus services, it makes those services feel normal rather than something only struggling students need.

Run Campaigns That Challenge Stigma

For many students, especially first-generation or high-achieving students, asking for help feels like admitting failure. Universities need to actively reframe the narrative around using campus resources—showing that tutoring, counseling, and career coaching are for *everyone*, not just those struggling.

A campus-wide campaign could include:

- Posters, digital screens, and social media graphics with messages like:
  - "Even the best students need tutoring—it's how they stay ahead."
  - "Talking to a counselor doesn't mean you're

struggling—it means you're smart about self-care."
    - "Career services isn't just for seniors. The earlier you start, the easier your job search will be."
- Having professors embed reminders in their syllabi or mention resources in class to help reduce stigma and increase usage.
- A "Resource Challenge" campaign where students are incentivized to check out different services and post about their experiences.

Build Community Through Digital and Social Channels

A strong sense of belonging can make the difference between a student who thrives and a student who quietly disengages. While in-person experiences matter, digital and social channels are as powerful—sometimes even more so. Students are already spending hours a day online, scrolling through social media and engaging in group texts. Universities that use these digital spaces to foster connection rather than just push out announcements can create a more engaged campus community.

Authenticity is everything. Students don't want to see stock photos of smiling students who may or may not even go to their school. They want real stories from real people. When institutions use social media to showcase unfiltered student voices—through takeovers, testimonials, or behind-the-scenes glimpses of campus life—it makes the university feel more like a home and less like an institution.

Beyond just storytelling, digital platforms should serve as conversation spaces. Universities that engage with students—replying to comments, hosting Q&A sessions, featuring student-led content—signal that they're listening. Community-driven initiatives, like student-run TikTok challenges, Discord groups for different academic interests, or Instagram Live events with faculty and advisors, can create digital gathering places where students feel seen and heard.

Digital platforms can bridge gaps for students who may not always feel represented in traditional campus settings. A commuter student or an online learner who might not always feel connected in person can find their niche in a well-run university forum or a group chat designed for their specific experience.

When done right, digital engagement helps students feel connected and supported—even when not physically on campus. And in an era where so much of student life happens online, that sense of digital belonging can be as meaningful as an in-person experience.

Our Moral Imperative

At the heart of every retention statistic is a student who took a leap and hoped they were making the right choice. Every student who leaves before finishing is someone whose dreams were put on hold and who might never return to complete their degree.

That's why marketing has to be more than a megaphone for recruitment. It must be part of the student experience from day one to graduation. We need to be as focused on helping students succeed as we are on getting them in the door in the first place.

Retention isn't an academic affairs problem. It's a marketing opportunity to shape how students experience your institution, not just how they enter it. Don't let your intentionality end once students are on board. Demonstrating that you understand and care about their needs is just as important with current students as with prospects. A great side effect of this approach is the creation of authentic ambassadors. Happy, engaged students naturally become your biggest advocates, sharing their pride and enthusiasm for your institution with others. They embody your brand and tell your school's story in ways no marketing campaign could.

Fixing all of these challenges may feel overwhelming. The day I wrote this, I talked to a colleague who admitted, "Sometimes, it's just easier to keep doing what we've always done in our silo rather than involve others." But that mentality is exactly what got us here in the first place.

The next chapter explores how to break down those silos and foster real, pain-free collaboration.

Insights and Impact Plan

Hype-Free Insights

- **Retention Should be a Marketing Priority:** Getting students in the door is only half the battle—helping them persist and graduate is just as important. Low retention and graduation rates don't just hurt students; they damage a university's reputation, rankings, and financial stability.
- **Students Are Overwhelmed by Disorganized, Transactional Communications:** Too many emails are sent

by too many different departments, which leads to email fatigue—students tune out and ignore important information. Marketing can help streamline and improve messaging so students receive **fewer but more meaningful** communications.
- **Proactive Communication Helps Students Navigate Challenges:** Timely, student-friendly emails or texts can guide students through common obstacles, and social media can play a role in normalizing struggles and reinforcing resilience.
- **Marketing Can Make Campus Resources More Visible and Reduce Stigma:** Many students don't use support services (like tutoring, mental health counseling, or career coaching) because they either don't know they exist or feel embarrassed to seek help. Framing services as something everyone uses, not just struggling students, can help encourage participation.
- **Building Community Through Digital and Social Channels Enhances Student Belonging:** Students spend much of their time online, so social media and digital spaces should be used to foster connection, not just push announcements.

Impact Plan

- **Gather student feedback** through focus groups or surveys to understand how communication strategies impact their experience.

- **Work with institutional research** to track retention metrics, engagement rates, and student satisfaction over time.
- **Conduct an email audit:** How many emails are students receiving from different departments? Are they redundant, overwhelming, or poorly timed?
- **Work with other campus units to bundle related messages** into weekly or bi-weekly digests instead of sending separate emails.
- **Work with campus services** to highlight free resources in a way that removes stigma.

Chapter 5
Busting Silos to Make Change

As a kid, my family spent fall weekends hiking in northern Minnesota. One crisp afternoon, we stumbled upon an abandoned barn with a towering, crumbling silo.

The silo was both fascinating and terrifying. Inside, the air was thick with dust. It was dark, damp, and disorienting—claustrophobic in a way that made my stomach turn.

I remember going into the silo and sneezing at all the dust in the air. It was dark, dank, and eerie—even more than the barn we explored. The roundness and the darkness were disorienting. And when I looked up, I felt dizzy. It was true tunnel vision.

Inside that silo, I lost my sense of the largeness of the world. I lost my view of the crystal blue sky. The stone walls blocked the sounds of my sisters and parents. The world narrowed to that small, stale tube.

Even decades later, I remember that suffocating sense of tunnel vision. Higher education silos may be less dusty (though I wouldn't bet on it), but they create the same effect—narrow perspectives, disconnection, and an inability to see beyond our immediate surroundings.

When we are siloed, our field of vision is limited to what is in that silo with us. We lose our perspective on what is happening outside the silo. We lose our connection with the other areas of the "farm." We are disoriented, disconnected, constrained. But because we have "grown up" in these silos and they are all we know, we think that is just the way it is. We don't know what we don't know. We can't see what we can't see. We can't experience what we can't experience. It's our only reality. And it's destructive toward progress.

A friend of mine once said that universities operate like a group of independent franchisees rather than as cohesive and unified institutions with shared visions and goals. We are divided in so many ways. By college. By division. By department. Even within departments, we find silos. The hierarchy of higher ed seems designed for these divisions.

And it makes sense. Earning a PhD can be a pretty solitary endeavor. Despite having classmates and mentors, crafting your dissertation is not a group project. And the sometimes cut-throat nature of obtaining a tenure-track job can lead to territoriality and isolation. And who runs our universities, typically? So many administrators rise from the faculty ranks having experienced the rigor of academia and the almost-hazing-like way we create PhDs. It's no wonder we operate the way we do.

Because we spend all day, every day, in our little slice of the university, we begin to feel like I did in that falling-down silo. We lose our sense of place and start to believe that the rest of the larger university world is irrelevant. If nothing else, we lose sight of our colleagues who are also working away in their own little worlds. We cannot hear outside voices. We cannot see that there is something bigger out there.

Now, imagine tearing those silos down. The view clears. We can see each other, hear each other, and work toward something bigger than ourselves—together.

Silos vs. Brands

What does this have to do with marketing?

Everything.

It isn't possible to tell an effective story from a silo. Without the context of the broader university world, our tales are incomplete. They rely only on the context that exists in that small tube. Of course, some people's silos might be larger than others. And some may have windows. But they are still constricting and leave us with limited vision. Even a clear glass silo would block out the voices of people we need to hear to be truly effective.

When we break down silos and embrace a collaborative mindset, we unlock the full potential of our institutions. True collaboration allows us to see the bigger picture and to connect disparate threads into a unified message that reflects the complexity and richness of our university communities. The stories we tell become richer, and our campaigns resonate more deeply. We are able to be truly effective.

The first thing we must do is recognize siloed thinking.

Me vs. We

When I hear words like 'I,' 'me,' and 'mine' on a college campus, my antennae go up. Nothing belongs to just one person, one unit, or one department. Everything—every initiative, every story, every decision—belongs to the institution and the students we serve.

We have the enormous privilege of being stewards of the "stuff" we do and the "stuff" we create. We are stewards of the brand and of the student experience. While we do have a responsibility to leverage our expertise to make our work the best it can be, we do not have the right to decide that our opinions alone are valuable. Branding is a team effort.

What are the benefits of synergy? There are so many. And I promise, they are all worth it.

Unified Storytelling

Working synergistically, we can be unified in our storytelling.

When I was at Miami University, we pulled together all of the directors of communications twice a month to talk about each area's overall content strategy. We built a massive document that everyone had access to and could see as stories came alive.

Let's say a communicator is writing about a grant a biology professor received to conduct cutting-edge research. Thanks to cross-campus collaboration, that story isn't just used on the department website. Perhaps the professor is an alumna—Alumni Relations can feature the story in its monthly newsletter. Or maybe the enrollment marketing team is looking for compelling content to share with prospective graduate students. Now, the story becomes part of the biology program's drip campaign.

Or consider a story about a student who had an amazing internship experience working for a professional sports team. Maybe that story was originally slated to appear on her department's blog. But perhaps she is also a student-athlete. Now, the athletics department can feature the piece on its website and in its newsletter. The writer, who might have expected only a handful of readers on the department blog, suddenly reaches a massive audience of tens of thousands.

The thing is, our students aren't just one thing. They are biology majors *and* dance minors. They are grad students *and* members of student organizations. They are English majors *and* volunteers at the local elementary school. They are whole people with whole stories that deserve a bigger platform.

Diverse Perspectives and Creativity

Another benefit of synergy is having diverse perspectives in our work. How many of us have made a blunder in our work because we didn't ask the right person for feedback? I know I have. And for every blunder I know about, I'll bet there are many more that just never came to my attention.

Our work gets stronger when there are more voices at the table. The chief marketing officer can't do this on her own. Neither can the president the, the provost, or any other individual on campus.

When we work in isolation—or even with just others who live in the same environment we do—we can't hear what's outside of us. We bumble into making comments that are culturally insensitive. We accidentally leave out an important fact. We oops our way into slighting someone.

But other voices are just good for telling us when we are about to mess up. They help make our work stronger.

Collaboration and Empathy

Collaboration requires empathy. Empathy is the key to understanding the perspectives of others and creating a culture where collaboration thrives. It requires us to actively listen to our colleagues' and stakeholders' challenges and priorities, even when they differ from ours. It allows us to step into their shoes to see the world through their lens and find common ground that connects their goals to ours.

When we empathize with our colleagues, we recognize that their priorities—whether in admissions, student affairs, or academic departments—are not obstacles to our work but vital pieces of the larger institutional puzzle.

Strategic Alignment and Vision

Synergy also allows us to be aligned toward a common vision and to make rapid progress toward that vision.

Picture a sled dog team. Sled dogs are highly trained animals. They love what they do, and they are darn good at it. One team can travel over 90 miles in a day while pulling 85 pounds each.

The reason they can get so far so quickly isn't just because they are well-trained. It's also because they are pulling together—and with alignment comes momentum.

If that team of sled dogs were all pulling in different directions, no matter how much effort they put in, the sled would barely budge. Without alignment, momentum stalls entirely. The sled bounces awkwardly in place, the team burns energy for no real progress, and frustration builds. Everyone works hard, but without direction, it leads nowhere except to poor morale and missed goals.

But when the team is aligned, they create momentum. Once the sled starts to move, every step forward becomes easier than the last. The same effort propels the sled faster and farther. It glides effortlessly over the snow. Miles seem to disappear, and before they realize it, the team has reached their destination.

Now, bring that analogy back to your marketing efforts. When your campus isn't aligned, energy is wasted in countless directions. Perceptions remain stagnant, your brand lacks impact, and progress feels like a distant dream. It's the equivalent of spinning in place—exhausting, frustrating, and ultimately fruitless.

But when alignment is achieved, momentum kicks in. Suddenly, every department and every initiative is pulling in the same direction. Progress accelerates as the collective effort becomes greater than the sum of its parts. Your brand story gains clarity, your outreach resonates, and results come faster and more effortlessly. With momentum, the once-daunting task of reshaping perceptions becomes not just possible but exhilarating.

Few schools master this. Imagine what it would mean for *your* university to lead the way—to harness alignment and momentum in a way that transforms your campus and the lives it touches. Imagine being the example others strive to emulate. It starts with everyone pulling together; the rest is the magic of momentum.

Intentional Actions

So, how do we take those first steps to work beyond our silos and build the synergy and momentum we need? It starts with intentional action and a commitment to rethinking old habits. Collaboration doesn't happen by accident. It's a deliberate process requiring a shift in mindset and operations. Start by setting the tone through meaningful engagement, particularly with voices that may have been historically excluded. These voices often provide the fresh perspectives needed to transform a siloed culture into one of true partnership.

This might mean contacting departments you don't typically interact with, such as IT, student affairs, or facilities management. These groups often hold valuable insights about the student experience or institutional needs that aren't immediately obvious from within the marketing or communications lens. Establish exploratory meetings where the only agenda is listening and identifying shared goals. Consider rotating leadership of these meetings to ensure everyone has a stake in the conversation.

If meetings feel too formal, start small. Drop by someone's office to brainstorm or invite a colleague to lunch to discuss how your work might intersect. Building these connections can feel awkward at first, especially if institutional silos have been entrenched for years, but collaboration isn't an innate skill. It's a muscle we develop over time; like any muscle, it grows stronger the more we use it.

Remember that cross-university team I mentioned in the introduction? In forming that group, I pulled in people from nearly every department on campus. But not just leadership. I also asked for administrative assistants and program associates to be part of the conversation. Think about the lobby of the financial aid office. The person at the front desk is privy to countless conversations students have while they wait for their appointments. Or the program associate who answers phone calls. He can relay frequently asked questions in a way that no director can.

To make collaboration stick, consider implementing centralized resources or shared tools that foster transparency and accessibility. A communal content calendar, for example, ensures that all teams know what others are working on, creating opportunities to identify overlaps and align messaging. Similarly, a shared project management system can track initiatives across departments, ensuring efficiency and minimizing duplicative efforts.

For more immediate collaboration, platforms like Slack or Microsoft Teams can act as virtual hubs where ideas flow freely. Create channels dedicated to storytelling, campaign brainstorming, or even cross-departmental shoutouts. These spaces help demystify the work others are doing and open doors to partnerships that may not have been obvious before. When everyone has access to what others are planning or producing, it becomes easier to see alignment opportunities—and harder to justify staying in your silo.

Reframing Success

Another critical step is reframing what success looks like. In higher ed, where departmental goals often take center stage, it's easy to fall into the trap of focusing solely on "your" project or hitting "your" metrics. While it's important to meet individual objectives, the reality is that no department exists in isolation. True success happens when the entire university advances—when the campaign contributes to a shared narrative, amplifying the institution's mission.

Reframing success requires a mindset shift: moving from a "me" perspective to a "we" perspective. Your work is part of a larger tapestry, one where the threads are interwoven, and each one strengthens the whole. For example, a beautifully told story about a groundbreaking research project isn't just a win for the department that published it; it's a win for the university as it reinforces the brand, engages alumni, and inspires prospective students.

When we celebrate wins, let's also celebrate collaboration. Highlighting examples of teamwork reinforces the value of working together and encourages others to seek out partnerships. Did two units join forces to create a campaign that reached more students than ever before? Make that collaboration the star of your internal communications. Did a member of the admissions team share a student success story that helped the alumni office craft a more compelling message? Shine a light on how that cross-departmental exchange made a measurable impact.

Elevating these collaborative successes requires intentionality. Build mechanisms for identifying and sharing these stories. Perhaps it's a regular feature in your internal newsletter or a spotlight at your monthly all-staff meetings. You might even consider creating awards that celebrate teamwork, such as a "Synergy Award" for initiatives that exemplify collaboration. At WSSU, our annual employee awards ceremony was designed explicitly to recognize efforts that involved multiple departments working together. Award nominations required at least two units to be involved in the project. This helped build that culture of collaboration.

It's also important to measure and communicate the ripple effects of collaboration. When two or more departments work together, the outcomes often go beyond what any single unit could achieve on its own. For example, a campaign that involves marketing and student affairs input might lead to higher student engagement and better alignment with institutional priorities. Be sure to quantify and share these outcomes—both the tangible (metrics, participation rates, revenue) and the intangible (enhanced relationships, improved morale).

Resistance to Change

Breaking down silos often meets resistance, and that resistance is both natural and predictable. People may fear losing control over their work or worry that collaboration will dilute their influence or resources. Others may be skeptical about the benefits of collaboration, dismissing it as an abstract ideal rather than a practical solution.

Acknowledging these fears is the first step to overcoming them. Resistance to change often stems from a fear of the unknown, so be sure to provide clarity and reassurance about the process. Transparency about the goals of collaboration and the steps involved will help alleviate anxiety. People need to know they are not being asked to give up their autonomy but to expand their impact by working together toward a greater purpose.

Trust is the foundation of any successful collaboration. Without it, people are more likely to hold back, fearing that their contributions may be undervalued or their efforts exploited. Building trust can be as simple as starting with low-stakes projects that allow teams to experience collaboration without significant risk. These early successes can demonstrate the value of working together and set the tone for larger initiatives. Open and frequent communication also reduces uncertainty. When everyone understands what's happening, why it matters, and how their input is being used, they are more likely to feel engaged. Recognizing the efforts of individuals and teams publicly fosters goodwill and encourages others to follow suit.

Shared goals are another essential element of overcoming resistance. Silos persist because different departments or teams often focus solely on their own objectives. By establishing shared goals that align with the broader mission of the institution, silos can begin to dissolve. Goals framed around student success, alumni engagement, or institutional growth resonate across units. Cross-departmental metrics, like increased student retention or improved graduation rates, can help align everyone's efforts toward the same outcomes.

Early wins can help address skepticism about collaboration and serve as proof points. Highlighting successful projects demonstrates that breaking down silos isn't just a theoretical exercise; it produces real, measurable results. Sharing success stories internally, such as a campaign that increased engagement or saved significant resources, reinforces the tangible benefits of collaboration. Data that quantify these outcomes lends further credibility to the value of working together. People respond to results, and the more examples of collaboration's effectiveness they see, the more likely they are to participate in the future.

"Baby" Steps

We often hear the phrase "baby steps" when talking about making progress, but I think we've got the imagery all wrong. When most people say "baby steps," they're picturing something small and cautious. But have you ever actually watched a baby take their first steps?

A baby doesn't tiptoe nervously into the world of walking. No, they stand up with determination—maybe a little wobble—but then they go for it. They lunge forward, arms outstretched, sometimes laughing, sometimes face-planting, but always moving. They don't second-guess themselves. They don't worry about whether they'll stumble. They just take the step.

And that's exactly the mindset we need when stepping into change. We have to move with the same fearless energy, the same excitement, and the same willingness to learn from the occasional fall.

Progress doesn't come from standing still, waiting until we feel 100% ready. It comes from stepping forward, trusting that even if we don't get it perfect right away, we're heading in the right direction.

The act of breaking down silos begins with these "baby steps," each fueled by empathy. Ask yourself: what small step can you take today to foster collaboration? Who can you invite to coffee to better understand their goals? Who might benefit from an invitation to share their perspective? These steps don't have to be monumental; they just need to be intentional.

Insights and Impact Plan

Hype-Free Insights

- **Silos in Higher Education Limit Progress:** Silos create a narrow, disconnected view, much like being inside a physical silo.
- **Breaking Down Silos is Essential for Effective Marketing:** Marketing and storytelling require a broad, institution-wide perspective.

- **A Shift from "Me" to "We" Thinking:** Effective branding and storytelling require collective stewardship, not isolated efforts. Success should be measured at the institutional level rather than by individual departments.
- **Intentional Steps to Overcome Silos:** Collaboration doesn't happen by accident—it requires deliberate action.
- **"Baby Steps" Toward Change:** Change doesn't require perfection—it starts with bold, fearless steps. Initiate conversations, invite others into the process, and amplify diverse voices to drive progress.

Impact Plan

- **Identify and Acknowledge Siloed Thinking:** Assess your own team's workflows—where are silos limiting collaboration? Listen for "I" and "mine" language in discussions and shift toward a collective "we" mindset. Encourage team members to recognize when they are operating in isolation.
- **Build Cross-Departmental Relationships:** Schedule regular meetings with other departments to discuss shared goals. Set up informal coffee chats or lunches with stakeholders to understand their priorities.
- **Create Shared Tools and Resources:** Develop a centralized content calendar to align messaging across campus. Use Slack, Microsoft Teams, or another collaboration platform for cross-departmental conversations.

- **Align Marketing and Communications with Institutional Goals:** Ensure that storytelling efforts align with the university's brand and mission. Use shared performance metrics that focus on institutional success rather than departmental wins.

Chapter 6
Facts Inform, Stories Transform

I'm a sucker for an emotional story. A soldier surprising his daughter at school after a long deployment? Tears. A neglected dog finally trusting its new guardian? More tears. A young woman meeting the man whose life she saved by donating an organ? Forget it—I'm sobbing into my coffee. Some stories don't just tug at the heartstrings; they play an entire symphony.

Why? The best commercials do that, too. One that stands out in my mind is the JB Whiskey ad (of all things). The three-minute ad takes viewers to rural Spain, where an older man quietly embarks on a secret mission: teaching himself how to apply makeup. At first, his purpose isn't clear. He locks himself in the bathroom, painstakingly applying lipstick and blush—each stroke uncertain but determined. The mirror reflects frustration, then quiet resolve. He visits the local drugstore, slipping past judgmental glances to buy eyeshadow, undeterred in his quiet mission.

The emotional payoff comes when his family arrives for Christmas dinner. The man takes his nineteen-year-old grandchild into the bathroom and puts his newfound skills to work. When the "son" emerges as a "daughter", her face beautifully made up, the moment is transformative. Her family embraces her in an outpouring of love and acceptance, leaving viewers moved by the grandfather's quiet yet powerful act of solidarity and support.

(I won't lie. I cried typing that. I cried, rewatching it. I'm still crying. And if I ever create something that powerful, I will retire happy.)

The emotional resonance in that story, which has no spoken words, is what takes the typical and makes it transformation.

Great stories exist everywhere—including on our campuses. In every classroom, on every quad, in every late-night study session, moments unfold that could move someone to tears and inspire action. But every so often, a story comes along that changes you, too.

Tony and Robert, a father and son duo, walked across the stage together at Radford University's graduation in May 2012. Their journey to that moment was anything but ordinary. Tony, born with a defective heart valve, faced significant physical challenges. Meanwhile, Robert, born with Stargardt's Disease, navigated life with limited vision, as the condition left him legally blind.

They decided to attend college together and became each other's greatest support system. Tony guided Robert around campus and read materials to him while Robert carried books for them both. When one faced discouragement, the other was always there to lift him up. They turned every obstacle into opportunity and proved that grit and teamwork can overcome any challenge.

As we planned the video and worked through the creative process, I found myself drawn to the layers of their journey: the way Tony's pride shone through when he spoke about his son, the way Robert's joy and determination lit up the room, and the way their story embodied so much of what higher education should be about—possibility and transformation.

As the video came together, I was struck by how storytelling could do something that facts and figures never could. It could create a connection. It could build bridges between people who might never meet but who could recognize something of themselves in Robert's journey or Tony's love. And it could remind all of us why we do what we do in higher education—to change lives.

Stories Transform

Storytelling is the beating heart of marketing. Stories like Tony and Robert's or the JB Whiskey ad remind us that storytelling is about emotion and shared humanity. Stories help make people feel seen and inspired.

Storytelling isn't some mysterious trick—it's a skill. It comes down to tapping into real human experiences and shaping them in a way that connects. The magic isn't in the words alone, but in uncovering what truly matters to your audience and crafting narratives that create impact.

As we move into this chapter, we'll explore the anatomy of storytelling—the techniques and strategies that elevate a story from transactional to transformational. Whether you're sharing a video, crafting a social media post, or presenting at a campus event, the principles of empathetic storytelling can take your message from ordinary to unforgettable.

The Science Behind Storytelling

Storytelling is a deeply ingrained human experience supported by science. Research from neuroscience to psychology shows why stories resonate powerfully with us. Here's a breakdown of what happens when we tell and hear stories and why they're so effective at capturing attention, evoking emotion, and driving action.

Stories Activate the Brain

Stories don't just capture attention—they light up the brain. When we hear statistics, only the language-processing centers activate. But a good story? That's a full-brain experience. A well-told narrative stimulates:

- **The sensory cortex:** When stories include vivid details (e.g., "the crisp crunch of autumn leaves"), our brain reacts as if experiencing those sensations.
- **The motor cortex:** Action words or descriptions (e.g., "she sprinted across the field") activate the parts of the brain associated with physical movement.
- **The emotional centers:** Emotional narratives trigger the amygdala, which processes feelings like joy, fear, and empathy.

This multi-sensory activation helps stories stick in our memory. It makes them far more engaging than raw data or abstract concepts.

Stories Trigger Emotional Responses

Emotion is the cornerstone of a good story. Neuroscience shows that when we connect emotionally to a narrative, our brains release oxytocin, often called the "love hormone." Oxytocin fosters trust, empathy, and a sense of bonding, which explains why stories effectively build relationships between brands and audiences.

Stories that evoke emotions like joy, sadness, or excitement don't just make us feel—they make us care. This emotional resonance is critical in decision-making, as people are likelier to act when they feel emotionally invested.

Stories Enhance Memory

Our brains are wired to remember stories better than isolated facts or figures. A study by Stanford University found that people are 22 times more likely to remember information when it's presented as part of a story. Why? Stories provide context, structure, and meaning, making information more memorable.

For example, statistics about graduation rates might be forgotten. But if paired with a student's personal journey, it becomes a story that sticks. The narrative framework helps the brain organize and recall details more effectively.

Stories Foster Empathy

Through neural coupling, our brains synchronize with the storyteller's. When you hear a story, your brain mirrors the emotions, thoughts, and experiences described as if you're living them yourself. This is why a powerful story can make us cry, laugh, or feel inspired.

Empathy is crucial in marketing and leadership because it deepens connection and trust. Stories help audiences see themselves in the narrative, fostering a sense of belonging and shared experience.

Stories Drive Action

Humans are hardwired to respond to stories with action. Researchers have found that when people feel emotionally engaged with a narrative, they're more likely to donate, volunteer, or make a purchase. This is because stories make abstract ideas tangible, turning "what if" into "what's possible."

For example, instead of just stating that scholarships help students, a story about a specific student whose life was transformed by financial aid makes the concept relatable and motivates support.

Stories Create Connection and Meaning

Anthropologists suggest that storytelling has been central to human survival, helping early societies share knowledge, build relationships, and make sense of the world. Today, stories still serve as tools for connection. They help us align our values with those of a brand, institution, or cause.

By framing information within a story, you move beyond mere facts to communicate meaning. This is particularly powerful in higher education, where decisions are often driven by logic (cost, programs, reputation) and emotion (belonging, aspiration, identity).

Why Empathy Matters in Storytelling

Stories are all about connection. They pull us in because they tap into emotions we all recognize—hope, excitement, fear, pride. When you tell a story that feels real, it sticks. It makes people think, *That's me. They get it.* That's what empathy does. It's the invisible thread that connects your institution's mission to someone's deepest hopes and fears.

Students, parents, and alumni aren't only looking for facts or stats. They want to feel like they belong, like your institution sees them for who they are and who they hope to become. Empathy-driven storytelling makes that connection possible. It builds trust. It shows authenticity. And in a crowded market where every college is shouting, "Pick us!" it's what sets you apart.

Here's a key distinction: there's transactional storytelling, and then there's transformational storytelling. Transactional storytelling delivers information. Transformational storytelling creates impact. One shares facts, the other sparks emotion. One aims to persuade, the other moves people to action.

Here's how to move from transactional to transformational storytelling:

Make the Audience the Hero

Nobody wants to hear you brag. Saying, "We're ranked in the top 10," might sound impressive, but it's all about you. Talk about the people you've helped instead. "Students like Sarah, who dreamed of becoming a nurse, chose us because we gave her the tools to turn her passion into a career. Today, she's on the front lines of healthcare, making a difference every day."

Now, who's the star of that story? It's Sarah. And that's exactly where the focus should be. Prospective students (and their parents) want to see themselves in the narrative. They don't care as much about your institution's achievements—they care about how those achievements will impact *them*.

Highlight Emotional Journeys, Not Just Outcomes

Stats are fine, but they're forgettable. Telling me that "90% of your graduates find jobs" isn't going to tug at my heartstrings. But tell me about Maria and how she pushed through sleepless nights and moments of doubt with the help of a mentor from your career services team. Share how that connection helped her land her dream job. Suddenly, it's not just a number; it's a story.

Outcomes are important, but the emotional journey to get there is what resonates. People connect with struggle, triumph, and perseverance. Share those details. Bring your audience along for the ride.

Use Real Voices and Authenticity

People see right through marketing speak. But tell them about Ahmed, who left everything he knew in Egypt to come to your campus, and how the friendships he made turned an unfamiliar place into a second home? That's a story that moves.

Authentic voices have power. They add credibility and humanity. Use quotes, videos, or even Instagram takeovers to let your students, alumni, and faculty share their experiences in their own words. People trust stories that feel real.

Get Specific

General statements are boring. "We have a state-of-the-art science center" might check the box, but it doesn't move anyone. Now imagine this instead: "When Jordan stepped into our new science lab for the first time, she felt like her future snapped into focus. 'This is where I'm going to help solve climate change,' she thought. And three years later, she co-authored her first peer-reviewed article on sustainability."

The details make it relatable. They turn a generic statement into a moment someone can picture and remember.

Connect to Shared Values

It's not enough to say, "We prioritize sustainability." That's a headline, not a story. Instead, talk about Alex, who launched a campus composting initiative that diverts thousands of pounds of waste yearly. Share Alex's motivation: "I wanted to leave the world better than I found it." That story inspires because it's rooted in values your audience likely shares.

And values are where real connections happen. They move your audience from saying, "That's nice," to thinking, "That's me."

Foster Empathy

When you share Liam's story—how financial aid meant more than just covering tuition, but proving to his siblings that their dreams were within reach—you're inviting people to imagine themselves in his shoes. That's empathy, and it's what makes stories stick.

Create Calls to Action with Heart

Instead of "Apply now," try this: "Take the first step toward a future you'll be proud of—apply today." It's a small change, but it makes a big difference. You're giving them a reason to believe in that action.

When you shift from transactional to transformational storytelling, you're building relationships. You're saying, "This is who we are. This is why we do what we do. And this is how you can be part of it." That's the kind of storytelling that gets attention and wins hearts. And isn't that the point?

Understanding Your Audience

If you don't understand your audience, you can't tell a story that will speak to them. It's that simple.

I don't mean just knowing their age ranges or their zip codes. I mean *really* knowing them. Understanding what keeps them up at night and what gets them out of bed in the morning. What drives them and what excites them? What are they hoping for and what challenges do they face?

Gaining that level of an understanding means gathering real insights through real conversations. You can't just make guesses. You have to actually sit down with representatives of your audiences and ask open-ended questions. Let them share their experiences in their own words.

Social listening is also a great way to gain insight. Like a sociologist, you can listen in on unfiltered conversations that will tell you volumes about what your audience cares about (and what frustrates them).

But never forget that your audience isn't a monolith. Every person in your community has their own perspectives and lived experiences. If you try to create a single narrative that speaks to everyone you will end up with something that doesn't truly connect with anyone. Instead, be sure you are showcasing a range of experiences, from a first-generation student navigating the college process to the adult learner balancing work, family, and school. Tell the stories that answer the questions they have or speak to the doubt they are experiencing: *am I college material? Will I fit in? Is this going to be too hard?*

The Art of Emotional Storytelling

At the heart of every great story is emotion. It's what makes people pay attention and care. Without an emotional core, a story is just facts strung together. But with emotion? A story becomes unforgettable.

So, where does emotion come from? You need to find the emotional heartbeat of your story—the part that connects to the audience on a deeply human level. Maybe it's a moment of triumph, like a student walking across the graduation stage as their family cheers. Or perhaps it's a struggle, like overcoming self-doubt or navigating unexpected challenges. The best stories have both. Think about the books you've read that have stuck with you. They are all about someone wanting or needing something and overcoming obstacles. Triumphs feel more powerful when they're earned.

Let's revisit that JB Whiskey ad I mentioned earlier. The commercial tells a powerful story with no spoken dialogue (a creative choice more universities should consider when producing video content). The absence of words allows the emotions to take center stage, making the message universally relatable and deeply impactful.

The narrative follows a grandfather as he embarks on a journey to show his presumably not openly transgender granddaughter that he wholeheartedly supports her. Along the way, he faces both internal and external challenges. He endures judgment from a shop owner as he buys makeup and risks ridicule from his wife as he practices applying it. He struggles with frustration as he tries and fails to perfect his application techniques. The tension builds as he works through his insecurities and societal pressures, highlighting internal growth and external resistance.

Finally, the grandfather triumphs. With a full face of expertly applied makeup, he looks in the mirror with pride and determination, ready to share what he's learned with his granddaughter.

The emotional climax comes when he stands beside her as she shyly steps into a family gathering as her true self. His thoughtful preparation and unwavering support send a clear message: no matter what, he will stand by her. That level of commitment is contagious, and the parents' quick, heartfelt acceptance reinforces the power of unconditional love and understanding.

This ad resonates on many levels because it reflects the power of vulnerability and empathy. It reminds us that meaningful connections are built through action, not just words. For universities, the ad serves as a blueprint for creating emotionally resonant content that shows, rather than tells, the values and commitments that define their communities. By crafting stories that speak directly to the heart, institutions can forge more profound, lasting bonds with their audiences.

Narrative Arcs

Even the most moving story needs a clear narrative arc. Start with an emotional hook. This is your chance to grab attention right out of the gate. It could be a moment of tension, joy, or even uncertainty—something that makes the audience think, *I need to hear how this ends.*

From there, craft your journey. Let the story unfold with all its layers: the struggle, the obstacles, the moments of doubt. But don't stop there. Bring your audience through to the growth and the triumph. People resonate with stories that reflect the rhythm of real life—the highs and the lows, the challenges and the victories.

For instance, think about telling the story of a transfer student. At first, he feels out of place and questions his decision to change schools. He sits quietly in a lecture hall, observing but not participating. Then, a moment of connection: a professor asks him to stay after class, intrigued by an idea he mentioned in a paper. They share a lively conversation that sparks his excitement and leaves him feeling seen.

Later, in the dining hall, he sits at a table alone, glancing at the groups of students laughing and chatting around him. He hesitates, unsure of how to join in. Then, someone from his class approaches, asking if she can sit with him. "You're in my chemistry lab, aren't you?" Soon, she calls over a friend, and before long, he's surrounded by a group of new friends, laughter and conversation filling the air.

This emotional arc—the initial struggle followed by the joy of belonging—resonates because it mirrors real experiences. It's genuine. It's relatable. It's human.

And the impact of a well-told story doesn't end with its

final scene. A powerful ending ties everything together emotionally. It leaves your audience inspired, moved, or thinking, *That could be me.*

Vonnegut's "Shape of Stories"

Kurt Vonnegut's "Shape of Stories" theory suggests that all stories follow familiar arcs—shapes that map out highs and lows in fortune over time. All marketing is storytelling, but the best marketing understands these arcs. By framing university messaging around recognizable story structures, universities can create campaigns that create emotional resonance.

The "Man in a Hole" story shape—where someone gets into trouble and climbs out— perfectly fits how universities can position themselves as the solution to a student's struggles. Prospective students often face uncertainty about their future: *what career path should I choose? How do I afford college? Will I fit in?* A well-crafted admissions campaign follows the "Man in a Hole" arc by acknowledging these concerns and presenting the university as the answer.

The "Cinderella" arc, where a character rises from hardship to success, is ideal for telling stories about students who overcome obstacles and thrive because of their education. This structure is powerful in alumni testimonials, fundraising appeals, and recruitment marketing.

A university could spotlight a student from an underserved community who, with the help of scholarships and mentorship, graduates and goes on to launch a successful startup or becomes a leader in their field. This arc also works for career outcomes campaigns, illustrating how an institution transforms students' futures.

The "Boy Meets Girl" arc—where something

extraordinary happens, is lost, then regained—fits well with messaging about the college experience. It mirrors the emotional journey of many students: excitement upon arriving on campus, challenges along the way (doubt, academic struggles, homesickness), and ultimately finding their place and purpose.

Vonnegut's "Shape of Stories" theory reminds us that facts and figures aren't enough; people connect with emotion and narrative.

Practical Techniques for Storytelling

Storytelling isn't just an art; it's a craft. When done well, it's magnetic. It pulls people in, makes them feel something, and leaves them with a lasting impression. But how do you get there? It starts with understanding the nuts and bolts of crafting a compelling story.

- **Structure Your Story for Maximum Impact**: Every great story follows a rhythm. First, grab attention. Start with something intriguing: a problem or an unexpected moment. Think of it as your "hook." Then, build the story. This is where the conflict or challenge unfolds, creating tension that keeps the audience invested. Finally, land the resolution. This doesn't have to mean a perfect, happy ending (though it can be!). It's about showing triumph or transformation.
- **Gather Real-Life Stories**: The best stories aren't created; they're discovered. The only way to find them is to be curious. Start talking to people. Ask students, alumni, and faculty about

their experiences. What moments defined their time at your institution? What challenges did they overcome? What surprised them? Open-ended questions like these often lead to the richest details. Don't stop at the obvious. Pay attention to what people mention in passing—those smaller moments that reveal something deeper. For instance, a student might casually mention how a professor checked in on them during a tough time. That's more than a nice anecdote. It's the heart of a story about community and care. Listen for those moments. A tossed-off sentence might reveal the compelling heart of a person's journey. Be willing to set aside your original questions and dig deeper when intrigued. If you're curious, chances are your audience will be, too.

- **Bring Stories to Life with Sensory Details:** The old adage from creative writing is true: "Show, don't tell." A story without details is like a painting without color. Sensory details are what make a story stick. They pull the audience into the moment, making them see, hear, and feel what the subject experienced. Instead of saying, "The student was nervous before their big presentation," say, "Her hands shook as she gripped the notecards, her heart pounding louder than the clock ticking on the wall." Suddenly, the moment comes alive. People don't just understand it—they *feel* it. And many of them will relate to it: the ultimate goal. But be careful not to overload. Pick a few key details that matter most. The smell of fresh-cut grass on move-in day. The rumble of applause in a packed lecture hall. The glow of a res hall room lamp during a late-night study session. It's these little things that make stories unforgettable.

How to Find Stories That Matter

Every institution has a wealth of stories waiting to be told. You just have to know where to look. These aren't the kind of stories that will drop into your lap. You'll need to listen closely and dig deeper to uncover the moments that reveal your institution's values and heart. Here's how to start finding those stories that truly connect.

- **Have Real Conversations:** Talking to people is one of the best ways to uncover meaningful stories. Sit down with people and ask open-ended questions that let them share their experiences in their own words. Look for moments of transformation, challenges they've overcome, or unexpected opportunities that shaped their journey. These conversations often uncover stories that go far beyond surface-level facts. Plus, they help build stronger relationships and show that you genuinely care about their experiences.
- **Step Into Their Shoes:** Sometimes, the best stories aren't told—they're observed. Spend time shadowing students or faculty to get a firsthand look at their daily lives. Walk alongside a first-year student juggling classes or sit in on a professor's groundbreaking research process.

Watch a student-athlete balancing their passion for sports with academic deadlines. This kind of immersion lets you experience your institution through their eyes, revealing moments of struggle, triumph, or connection that might not come up in an interview.

- **Host Storytelling Sessions**: Create spaces where people feel comfortable sharing by hosting storytelling workshops or casual meetups where students, faculty, and staff can share their experiences. This can be especially powerful for elevating unheard voices—underrepresented groups, quieter personalities, or people who don't usually step forward to share.
- **Keep an Eye on Social Media**: Social media is a treasure trove of stories. People are constantly posting about milestones, friendships, challenges, and moments of pride. Watch for posts that align with your institution's mission or values, then reach out to learn more. It could be a student's viral project or an alumna's heartfelt reflection on their time at your school. Always ask for permission before expanding on someone's post, and be sure to credit and thank them for sharing.
- **Use Surveys to Spot Trends**: Surveys are great for identifying broad themes or trends within your community. While they may not yield fully formed stories, they often highlight experiences worth digging into. Follow up with respondents who share something particularly moving or unique.

- **Tap Into Campus Networks**: Your departments and programs are natural hubs for stories. Contact faculty for details about innovative research or ask student leaders about impactful initiatives. Alumni offices, student organizations, and even campus facilities teams often have insights into individuals or events that deserve a spotlight.
- **Attend Events With a Story-Seeker's Mindset**: From athletic games to performances and fundraisers, campus events are full of potential stories. Watch for standout moments or hear memorable anecdotes shared during speeches. Events often bring out the best in people—their determination, their joy, their pride in belonging.
- **Make Sharing Easy**: Create a simple way for people to submit their stories. Whether it's a form on your website, a section in your newsletter, or a prompt on social media, encourage your community to share. You can even suggest themes like "moments of belonging" or "how I overcame a challenge" to get the ball rolling.
- **Don't Overlook the Everyday:** Not every great story comes from a big event or milestone. Often, the most authentic, relatable stories are found in small, everyday moments—a professor staying late to help a struggling student or friends cheering each other on during finals. Pay attention to the little things happening in hallways, dining areas, and classrooms.

Insights and Impact Plan

Hype-Free Insights

- **Emotion Transforms, Facts Inform.** The heart of compelling storytelling lies in its ability to evoke emotion. Facts and figures inform, but emotional narratives leave a lasting impact.
- **From Transactional to Transformational Storytelling:** Transactional storytelling focuses on surface-level facts and features, centering the institution. Transformational storytelling centers the audience as the hero, explores emotional journeys, and emphasizes the "why" behind the story.
- **The Power of Emotional Storytelling:** Emotional arcs—moments of struggle followed by triumph—create relatable and unforgettable narratives. Authenticity is key; focus on real experiences and let genuine emotions shine through.
- **Science Validates Storytelling:** Stories engage multiple areas of the brain, triggering emotional responses and enhancing memory. By activating oxytocin and fostering empathy, storytelling builds trust and inspires action.
- **Audience Understanding is Critical**: Truly impactful storytelling stems from knowing your audience's struggles, hopes, and questions. Techniques like social listening, honest

conversations, and surveys uncover the human experiences behind data points.
- **Storytelling is an Ongoing Craft**: Great stories don't happen by accident. They require intentionality, authenticity, and constant discovery. Through storytelling, institutions can inspire trust, build lasting connections, and showcase their transformative impact.

Impact Plan

- **Find and Elevate Hidden Stories:** Host storytelling workshops, engage in social listening, and connect with your campus community to uncover meaningful narratives.
- **Craft with Empathy:** Always ask: how will this story make the audience feel? Let emotion guide the tone, structure, and details of your narrative.
- **Balance Platforms and Formats:** Adapt your storytelling to suit different platforms while maintaining authenticity. Use micro-stories for social media, rich website narratives, and videos to capture emotion.
- **Test and Refine Stories:** Share drafts of stories with representative audiences. Gather feedback to ensure resonance, clarity, and relatability.

Chapter 7
Responding to Crisis with Care

Four weeks into my first role as chief communications and marketing officer at Winston–Salem State University, the unthinkable happened. A fatal shooting on campus with the gunman at large. A multi-hour lockdown. Students stranded in residence halls, alumni unable to leave a campus party, parents desperately refreshing their phones for updates. And me, jolted awake by an emergency alert followed almost immediately by a call from the deputy chief of police.

My heart began to race. This was my first lockdown and my first on-campus shooting as a chief marketing and communications officer. The weight of the situation hit me like a freight train. While I had crisis response experience from previous roles and had participated in tabletop exercises, nothing fully prepared me for the reality of that night.

To make things more challenging, I hadn't been in the role long enough to meet everyone in the emergency operations center. Meanwhile, my media relations director had his cell phone silenced, and I didn't have all his media contacts loaded into my devices. On top of that, my second-in-command was due to have a baby in five days.

While she offered to come to the EOC to assist me, I told her, "Absolutely not."

Inside, I was panicking. My heart pounded. My mind raced. But on the outside? I was steady. Calm. In control. Because in that moment, my colleagues needed reassurance. If I cracked, so would their confidence in my ability to handle the crisis.

To handle the logistics, I leaned heavily on the emergency management director, who patiently walked me through the alert system. When crafting messages, though, I relied on empathy.

With empathy as my guide, I imagined what it must feel like for students confined to their residence halls, unsure of what was happening; for alumni stranded on campus, unable to return home; and for parents miles away, anxiously refreshing their phones for updates and wondering if their child was safe. What would I want to hear in their position? How could I convey both critical information and reassurance? Those questions guided me as I drafted updates, doing my best to strike the right tone and share what I knew with transparency and care.

The night was a blur of emergency alerts, hurried conversations, and a phone that never stopped ringing. But beyond the chaos, something else stayed with me: how people responded. The gratitude, the trust, the way transparency mattered in those tense moments. And that's when I realized that crisis response can be a defining moment for a university's brand.

In the days that followed, I was struck by the response from our community. People stopped me as I crossed campus to express their gratitude for the information I shared and how it had been communicated. Students posted on social media that they felt supported and well-informed. Parents called and thanked us for keeping them looped in throughout the crisis.

While there was no undoing the heartbreaking loss of a young life that night—something that still haunts me—I found solace in knowing we had provided a sense of clarity and care during a dark and chaotic moment. In the face of tragedy, I learned one of the most important lessons of my career: when you lead with empathy, you can make even the most challenging situations a little more bearable.

Crisis Response as a Differentiator

A crisis is a spotlight. It's a moment to show (not just claim) what your institution truly values. While some schools might scramble to spin PR statements, those who lead with empathy set themselves apart. Why? Because empathy shows you care about the people you serve. That's what sticks with people long after the dust settles.

When a crisis hits, everyone is watching. Students, parents, faculty, alumni, and even unconnected social media commentators are all waiting to see how you'll react. It's not *what* you do that matters, but *why* you're doing it. People can tell when a response is driven by damage control versus genuine care. Trust me. I have been in situations when voices advocating for "spin" have defeated mine. The reaction was predictable and swift: deep cynicism.

Picture the kind of email most institutions might send out after a safety incident. It's straightforward: "Here's what happened. Here's what we're doing." It gets the job done. But it's sterile. Functional, sure, but also devoid of any emotion. It doesn't acknowledge the real fears people might feel. And in moments like that, an email like this can come across as indifferent—or worse, detached.

143

Now imagine a message that starts with heart, with humanity. Something like: "We know today's events have shaken our community. If you're feeling anxious or uncertain about what comes next, you're not alone. We're here for you. Support is available, and we will get through this together." It's the same basic information, but the tone shifts everything. It's no longer just a statement; it's an acknowledgment of the people behind the incident. It tells them: "We see you. We care. You're not alone."

People need to feel like their institution understands the emotional weight of what they're going through, especially in a crisis. That kind of empathy builds connection. It shows that leadership isn't just checking boxes or covering their bases—they lead with care.

When you respond with humanity, people notice. They feel the intent behind the words. That's what makes the difference between a message that's skimmed and one that sticks. Between a quickly forgotten response and one that strengthens trust, even in the toughest of times.

Building Trust That Lasts

Empathy doesn't just calm a crisis—it builds trust that lasts. Every crisis response sends a message. Will people remember your institution as one that stepped up with care? Or as one that sent cold, corporate statements?

When universities act with humanity—offering emergency housing after a natural disaster, ensuring students feel supported in the wake of a tragedy—they aren't just managing a crisis. They're proving, in real time, that their values are more than just words.

A university that jumps into action after a natural disaster—perhaps by offering emergency housing and mental health resources—sends a loud and clear message: We've got your back. Or consider a financial aid snafu. A defensive response might say, "We're investigating." (Yawn.) But an empathetic one? "We understand you are disappointed/upset/frustrated. Here's what happened, how we're fixing it, and who you can contact for immediate help." (These messages are a key moment when busting the silo between communications and legal is key. You will want to work together on responses that express empathy but don't lead to potential liability.)

That trust ripples. Alumni feel more connected. Parents rave about how the school stepped up. Prospective students hear the stories and think, "That's the kind of place I want to be." Suddenly, your response shapes your institution's reputation in a way that no marketing campaign ever could.

Empathy-driven responses have a way of sticking in people's minds (and hearts). When you lead with care, those moments don't just fade into the background. They become part of your institution's story.

Maybe it's a parent telling their friends how your school handled a campus emergency with transparency and compassion. Perhaps it's a student sharing on social media how the university made them feel supported after a major policy change. These anecdotes become testimonials.

And it's not only your stakeholders who notice. Media outlets love a good story about a university stepping up in a crisis. Compassionate action, whether opening dorms for evacuees or sending mental health counselors to help students, makes for better headlines than a dry, "official" statement ever will. That kind of coverage restores confidence and elevates your brand.

Where Values Meet Strategy

Crises reveal who you really are. You can claim to be a community-driven, values-based institution, but your actions in challenging moments make people believe it. Empathy is a strategic advantage. When you prioritize people over optics, you're building a reputation that outlasts the crisis. Stakeholders remember how you made them feel when things were hard. Were they seen, supported, and valued? Or did they feel like just another name on a spreadsheet?

In a crowded higher ed market, where everyone is shouting the same buzzword—"community," "inclusion," "student-focused"—the institutions that actually live those values stand out. Empathy-driven crisis response is a smart strategy. It's what turns crises into opportunities and institutions into beacons of care and humanity.

Acknowledging Emotions: The First Step to Resolution

When a crisis hits, you can end up focused on controlling the narrative or crafting a polished response. But it's essential to understand the people impacted—their emotions, questions, and concerns—and respond to them with care and clarity.

No two stakeholders experience a crisis the same way. Students might feel scared or unsure, especially if their safety, future plans, or sense of community are at stake. On the other hand, parents are likely to feel protective, searching for clear answers about how their child is affected. Faculty and staff often face a dual burden, balancing their personal worries with professional responsibilities. Alumni, deeply tied to the institution's reputation, may wonder how the crisis reflects on the university's values. And board members often grapple with high-stakes concerns about how the situation could affect the institution's reputation, finances, or alignment with its mission.

Then there's the surrounding community, which might ask entirely different questions. Will this hurt the local economy? Does it impact area safety? Does it damage the institution's relationship with the community?

The thread that ties all of these groups together is emotion. Fear, frustration, confusion, and even anger are natural responses during a crisis. Those feelings are valid. They deserve to be heard and acknowledged. Without that acknowledgment, no amount of carefully worded statements or strategic plans will resonate. Empathy is the bridge that turns crisis response into meaningful connection.

Recognizing and Validating Emotions

Validating emotions is an essential cornerstone of empathetic communication during a crisis. By validating emotions, you show stakeholders that they're valued as human beings and not just an audience to be managed.

Emotions drive how people perceive and respond to a crisis. When stakeholders feel their emotions are dismissed or ignored, their fear or anger often intensifies, making it harder for your messaging to land. On the other hand, when people feel understood and acknowledged, they're more likely to engage constructively, even under challenging circumstances.

Validation doesn't mean agreeing with every perspective. It's about showing that you understand and respect how someone feels. This can be done through:

- **Acknowledgment:** Start by naming the emotions people are likely feeling. This shows that you're tuned in to their experience.

Example: "We understand this news may be upsetting, especially for those directly impacted. Your well-being is our priority, and we're here to ensure you feel supported and informed."

- **Empathy Statements:** Express empathy for their situation in a sincere way. Avoid generic phrases and focus on the specific context.

Example: "We realize this policy change may have caught you off guard and raised questions about how it impacts you. Please know we are here to answer your questions and address any concerns you have as we move forward."

- **Reassurance Without Overpromising:** Validation doesn't mean you have to have all the answers. Sometimes, reassurance is simply letting people know you're listening and working toward a solution.

Example: "We know how disruptive today's system outage has been for students, faculty, and staff. Our IT team is working around the clock to resolve the issue, and we will provide regular updates as we make progress."

Tailoring Validation for Different Stakeholders

Validation isn't one-size-fits-all. Different groups will experience a crisis uniquely, and your approach should reflect that.

- **Students:** Students might feel anxious, scared, or even angry, especially if their daily routines or long-term goals are disrupted. Validation for students could sound like this: "We know that this situation may feel overwhelming and may leave you with questions about what's next. We're here to provide guidance and ensure you feel supported."
- **Parents:** Parents often bring protective instincts, worrying about their child's safety and future. Validation for parents might sound like: "We understand that you're concerned about your child's well-being, and we want to provide the clarity and reassurance you need during this time."
- **Faculty and Staff:** Faculty and staff may feel uncertainty about their roles, responsibilities, or job security. Validation could look like this for them: "We recognize the unique challenges this situation creates for our employees, and we are committed to supporting you as we navigate this together."
- **Alumni and Community Members:** These stakeholders often feel connected to the institution's reputation and values. For them, validation might sound like: "We understand how important [Institution Name]'s reputation is to our alumni and community. Please know that we are working to address this issue with integrity and transparency."

Tailored Validation for Board Members

Board members hold a unique position during a crisis. They're leaders invested in the institution's reputation and long-term stability. Crises often trigger a mix of emotions for board members: anxiety about how the issue will reflect on the institution, pressure to ensure appropriate action is taken, and concern about the broader implications for finances, governance, and strategy. Validating their emotions means acknowledging these pressures while reinforcing their role as trusted advisors.

I strongly urge university leaders to have messages to their boards come directly from the president (or another senior leader if the crisis involves issues with the president). Here are some examples of ways you can validate the feelings of board members:

- **Acknowledging Their Concern for Reputation**: "I understand that this situation raises concerns about the institution's reputation and the impact it could have on our stakeholders. Please know that protecting and strengthening our standing remains a top priority as we navigate this issue."
- **Recognizing Their Strategic Perspective**: "I know that as board members, you are focused on the immediate response and the long-term implications of this crisis. Your insights and guidance are invaluable as we work through these challenges."
- **Validating Their Leadership Role**: "I recognize the unique pressures that come with your leadership role, particularly during

challenging times like these. Your support and direction are critical to ensuring we respond effectively and honestly."
- **Acknowledging Their Desire for Clarity**: "I understand the importance of fully informing you about this situation. We are committed to providing regular updates and ensuring you have the information you need to make strategic decisions."
- **Recognizing Their Emotional Investment:** "I know this issue may feel personal, given your deep connection to [Institution Name] and its mission. Your passion for the institution drives us to address this issue thoughtfully and thoroughly."

Validation isn't rushing to take the blame or making promises you can't keep. It's showing compassion, demonstrating understanding, and creating space for open, honest communication.

When Validation Goes Wrong

It's worth noting that validation must be authentic. Insincere statements or attempts to dismiss emotions with empty platitudes can backfire, making people feel unheard or manipulated. For example:

- Avoid vague reassurances like, "Everything will be fine." If stakeholders feel that "fine" is far from reality, this can feel dismissive.
- Don't gloss over emotions with overly optimistic spins, such as, "We see this as an opportunity."

This might work in a team-building exercise, but it can feel like spin in a moment of crisis.
- Never rush to solutions before acknowledging the emotional weight of the situation. Jumping straight to "fix-it" mode can make people feel like their feelings are being brushed aside.

Responding with Transparency and Accountability

When a crisis or significant issue arises, stakeholders don't need you to be perfect. They need you to be honest. They want clarity, accountability, and a plan for moving forward. A thoughtful and transparent response shows respect for those impacted and reinforces your institution's commitment to its values. At its core, an empathetic approach ensures that your response is less focused on optics or damage control and more focused on people.

The first step in any effective response is to acknowledge the issue directly. Downplaying or spinning the situation might seem like a way to protect your institution in the short term, but in the long run, it erodes trust and credibility. People are looking for transparency. That means facing the problem head-on, being upfront about what you know, and being transparent about what remains uncertain.

I know what you might think: "Our legal team would never let us take this approach." And you're not alone. Striking a balance between expressing accountability and protecting your institution from liability is one of the most challenging aspects of crisis communication. It's a nuanced dance, but it's not impossible. With careful language you can address stakeholder concerns while maintaining the safeguards your institution needs.

Consider these examples of how to find that balance:

- **Acknowledge the issue without admitting fault prematurely:** "We're aware of the concerns raised and are taking them seriously. We've launched a review to understand what happened and will share updates as soon as we have them."
- **Express accountability while focusing on solutions:** "We recognize that this process has caused frustration for many members of our community, and we're committed to making improvements to ensure this doesn't happen again."
- **Highlight the next steps to demonstrate action:** "To address these concerns, we've formed a task force that will review our policies and recommend changes to strengthen our practices moving forward."

Share the Process

Transparency requires showing people what you're doing to fix the problem. Stakeholders aren't just waiting for an apology. They want to know you have a plan. They need to see that you're taking tangible, concrete steps to address the issue and that you're serious about making things right.

When you take the time to explain what actions you're taking and why, it helps people feel reassured. It minimizes speculation and prevents rumors from filling the silence. Plus, it shows that you're not brushing things under the rug. You're committed to open, honest communication.

Sharing your plan builds trust. People want to know

what's happening, how long it might take, and how they'll stay informed.

How to Share the Process Effectively:

Outline Immediate Actions: Let stakeholders know what you're doing to address the problem. Immediate actions demonstrate that the institution is aware of the issue and taking swift, decisive steps to mitigate the impact.

Example: "We have partnered with an independent auditor to review the circumstances surrounding this incident and are implementing additional security measures to ensure it does not happen again."

Set Expectations for Next Steps: Provide a clear roadmap of what happens next, including the measures being implemented and the outcomes you're working toward. This helps stakeholders feel informed and reduces uncertainty.

Example: "Over the next two weeks, we will review our policies and procedures fully and share a summary of the findings with our community."

Provide Timelines Where Possible: While you may not have all the answers immediately, giving stakeholders a sense of when they can expect updates or resolution builds confidence. Be realistic – overpromising and underdelivering can damage credibility.

Example: "We will provide a detailed report on our findings within 90 days and update you monthly on our progress."

Commit to Regular Updates: Transparency is an ongoing process. Regular updates keep stakeholders engaged and informed even if the situation remains unresolved. Consistent communication shows that you're prioritizing the issue and working toward resolution.

Example: *"We will provide weekly updates on the status of this investigation, which will be shared via email and posted on our website."*

Be Clear About Accountability: Transparency also means being clear about who is responsible for addressing the issue and what systems are being implemented to prevent future occurrences. This level of detail reassures stakeholders that you're fixing the immediate problem and tackling its root causes.

Example: *"To ensure accountability, we have established a task force that will report directly to the president's office and provide recommendations for systemic improvements."*

Listen and Adjust: Sharing the process isn't a one-way street. Encourage feedback and be prepared to adjust your approach as you learn more about stakeholder concerns and needs.

Example: *"We want to hear from you. Please share your thoughts and concerns through our dedicated feedback form so we can ensure our response meets your needs."*

Listening and Engaging Proactively

When a crisis strikes, communication can't be a one-way street. It's not enough to simply push out updates or deliver polished messages. You also need to create dialogue opportunities and actively listen to stakeholders. Effective issues management requires more than just speaking; it demands real engagement. Proactive listening is how you uncover what's not being said in a crisis. It helps you identify gaps in your response, rebuild trust, and, most importantly, show your community that their voices matter.

Create Opportunities for Feedback

Establishing clear channels for feedback is critical to understanding the full impact of a situation. Feedback mechanisms give stakeholders a chance to share their concerns and provide your institution with insights that can refine and improve your response.

Host Listening Sessions: Create spaces where stakeholders can directly share their concerns and questions. These can be virtual or in-person; having a neutral facilitator can help ensure everyone feels comfortable speaking up.

Example: Host a town hall for students and staff after a controversial policy change. Let stakeholders voice their frustrations and provide direct answers to their questions.

Use Anonymous Surveys or Feedback Forms: Sometimes, people hesitate to speak up out of fear of judgment or repercussions. Anonymous feedback channels allow stakeholders to share their honest perspectives.

Example: After a campus safety incident, send a survey asking, "What are your main concerns about safety, and what improvements would you like to see?"

Engage Key Stakeholder Groups: Bring representatives from different constituencies, such as student leaders, faculty committees, parent associations, or alumni councils, into focused conversations. This approach ensures diverse voices are heard and builds collaborative solutions.

Example: Meet with faculty leaders to discuss how the crisis affects morale and productivity and gather suggestions for support strategies.

Designate a Compassionate Response Team

In a crisis, every interaction is a chance to show who you are. Whether it's a worried parent emailing about their child's safety, a student expressing fear on social media, or a staff member seeking clarity, how you respond matters. You need to show a willingness to help. That's where a Compassionate Response Team comes in.

Think of this team as your institution's emotional first responders. They're there to answer questions and share updates, listen, acknowledge emotions, and provide support when people need it most. In the middle of a crisis, people don't just want facts—they want to feel seen and heard.

When a crisis hits, communication channels get flooded. Emails pile up. Social media lights up. Phone lines are jammed. It's overwhelming and impossible for one person —or even one team—to handle it all. A Compassionate Response Team spreads the responsibility across departments, ensuring every message gets a thoughtful and timely reply.

Admissions staff can step in to address worried calls from prospective families. Financial aid officers can tackle questions about scholarships or deadlines. Faculty representatives can help students navigate academic adjustments. Counseling staff can provide emotional support or connect people to mental health resources. Everyone plays a role, and together, the team ensures no one falls through the cracks.

These personal touches add up. Every response—a social post, an email, or a phone call—builds trust. It reminds people that behind the institution are actual humans who care. A personal reply stands out in a world where automated messages and generic statements are the norm. It shows you're there for your community.

Best Practices for a Compassionate Response Team

- **Empower the Team with Training:** Empathy doesn't come naturally to everyone; crisis situations can be emotionally charged. Provide team members training on active listening, de-escalation techniques, and crafting empathetic responses. Help them understand the nuances of responding in a way that validates emotions while maintaining professionalism.
- **Centralize Communication Guidelines:** To ensure consistency, create a response guide with key messaging points, FAQs, and tone recommendations. The guide should emphasize compassion, transparency, and clarity while leaving room for personalization.
- **Leverage Technology Thoughtfully:** Equip the team with tools to track and manage inquiries, such as a shared inbox, CRM system, or social media monitoring platform. These tools ensure that nothing falls through the cracks while allowing team members to collaborate effectively.
- **Set Clear Protocols:** Define roles and responsibilities within the team to avoid confusion. For example, designate who responds to social media inquiries versus hotline calls or

outline escalation paths for particularly sensitive cases.
- **Follow Up and Follow Through:** Compassionate responses shouldn't end with a single reply. If someone reaches out with a complex issue, follow up to ensure they've received the support they need. For example, if a student asks about accommodations during a crisis, check back in a week to see if the adjustments are working for them.

During my time at WSSU, a tragedy struck when a student lost his life over the summer break. As the university's spokesperson, I addressed the media to convey our community's profound sadness. Soon after, I received a call from the student's grieving father, who had looked up my number with questions about the next steps.

Over several phone calls, some lasting more than an hour, I supported him through the difficult process of retrieving his son's belongings and obtaining the paperwork necessary to discharge student loans. I provided a compassionate ear and ensured he had a single point of contact throughout this painful time. If he needed answers, I found them and called him back. I didn't just pass him off to someone else.

A few weeks after everything was resolved, I made a final call to check on him. His gratitude was deeply moving. He shared how much that follow-up meant to him and said my compassion had helped him endure the worst experience of his life. He told me he would always speak highly of WSSU as a place that actually cares. That conversation has stayed with me, reminding me of the impact kindness and compassion can have in times of heartbreak.

Recovering from a Crisis with Empathy

The immediate response to a crisis might get the spotlight, but the recovery process is where the real work happens. This is the phase where your institution's character is revealed. Handled thoughtfully, recovery can turn a difficult moment into an opportunity for stronger relationships with your community. Here's how to approach recovery with intention and care.

- **Step 1: Acknowledge the Impact.** Recovery begins with acknowledging the crisis and its lingering effects on your stakeholders. People's emotions often peak in the aftermath as they process what happened and its implications. Failing to address this stage can make your initial response seem hollow or insincere. Express appreciation for those who stepped up or demonstrated patience during the crisis. Show empathy for those still grappling with the aftermath. Acknowledge their feelings and commit to supporting them through the process.
- **Step 2: Provide Ongoing Transparency:** Transparency doesn't stop when the crisis subsides. Stakeholders expect updates and evidence that promises made during the crisis are being fulfilled. Regular communication helps maintain trust and keeps your community engaged in the recovery process. Keep stakeholders informed about the steps being taken and milestones achieved. If challenges arise, address them head-on. Transparency

about setbacks reinforces trust by showing accountability. Set clear expectations for when stakeholders can expect updates or resolutions.
- **Step 3: Engage Stakeholders in the Recovery Process:** Recovery isn't something you do *to* your community. It's something you do *with* them. Involving stakeholders in the process rebuilds trust and fosters a sense of shared ownership. Form committees with diverse representatives—students, parents, faculty, staff, and alumni—to provide input and oversight on recovery efforts. Offer spaces for stakeholders to reflect, share feedback, and ask questions as recovery progresses. Regularly check with stakeholders to assess whether recovery efforts meet their needs.
- **Step 4: Implement Long-Term Changes:** Crises often reveal underlying weaknesses or systemic gaps that must be addressed. Recovery is an opportunity to tackle these issues with thoughtful, sustainable improvements. Establish measurable goals, clear timelines, and accountability mechanisms for recovery efforts. Make lessons learned part of your institution's DNA by embedding them into policies, training, or cultural practices.
- **Step 5: Celebrate Progress and Reinforce Values:** As recovery progresses, acknowledge milestones and highlight how the process aligns with your institution's core values. Done thoughtfully, these celebrations demonstrate your commitment to growth while maintaining empathy for those still affected. Share successes

in a way that reflects the seriousness of the crisis while showing progress. Recognize the individuals and groups who played a key role in recovery.

Insights and Impact Plan

Hype-Free Insights

- **Acknowledging Emotions:** Addressing stakeholder feelings—whether fear for safety, frustration over disruptions, or concern about damage to the university's reputation—demonstrates care and respect.
- **Transparency Builds Trust**: Stakeholders don't expect perfection but demand honesty. Transparent communication includes admitting what is known, what remains uncertain, and what steps are being taken to resolve the situation. Avoiding spin or downplaying the issue is essential for maintaining credibility.
- **Tailored Messaging for Diverse Stakeholders:** Each group—students, parents, faculty, alumni, board members, and the broader community—has unique concerns and perspectives. Craft messages that reflect their specific needs and experiences, from reassuring students about their safety to addressing board members' strategic concerns.
- **Action Over Apologies:** While acknowledging mistakes is vital, the tangible

steps taken to address and resolve a crisis truly rebuild trust. Share immediate actions, outline long-term plans, and provide regular updates to show stakeholders their concerns are being taken seriously.
- **Engaging Stakeholders Proactively:** Crisis communication should be a two-way street. Hosting listening sessions, inviting feedback through surveys, and engaging advisory groups can provide valuable insights and demonstrate a commitment to collaborative problem-solving.
- **Recovery as an Opportunity for Growth:** Trust is solidified in the recovery phase. Acknowledge the lingering impact of the crisis, share progress updates, and involve stakeholders in shaping the path forward. Turn lessons learned into institutional improvements to prevent future issues.

Impact Plan

- **Review Your Templates:** Review your existing templates and holding statements to ensure that they validate the emotions that may be felt in a crisis. If you don't have templates, create them now.
- **Empower a Compassionate Response Team**: Identify staffing and train them to respond empathetically and consistently across all communication channels.

Chapter 8
Accessibility: The Real Competitive Edge

I'll admit it—accessibility wasn't always on my radar. Not because I didn't care but because I didn't know enough to truly understand its importance. I wasn't ignoring it but wasn't leading the charge either. That all changed during my time at Radford University. Back then, I was heading up web strategy, confident I was doing a solid job. But one conversation caused my perspective to shift completely, and I realized there was a whole dimension to my work that I had been overlooking. It was a wake-up call and the start of a transformation in how I approached everything I did.

The department I led was part of Information Technology, and my office was housed in the central Division of Information Technology suite. One day, the director of Technology Support Services walked into my office, clearly frustrated. "We've got a problem," he said. He explained that a blind faculty member was struggling because departments across campus sent mass emails as JPG images—emails with no text, just graphics with words baked into the image.

These emails might as well have been blank sheets for

someone using a screen reader. She could not know if the messages were important, time-sensitive, or critical to her work.

Every time an important email landed in her inbox, she had to call someone just to know what it said. Every. Single. Time. Imagine that—needing a second person just to access information that everyone else could read instantly. That's exclusion.

"Is there something you can do?" my colleague asked.

That question sparked a journey. I won't lie; it wasn't a quick fix. But that moment helped me see how critical accessibility is—and how often it's overlooked. I worked with our Office of Disability Services to draft an email policy requiring all campus communications to meet accessibility standards. But we didn't stop at rules. We added accountability measures: offices violating the policy twice would lose the ability to send campuswide emails until they did a remediation training. (I will say that the "appropriately assertive" email they got from me after the first offense was usually enough to scare them into compliance. I may be nice, but I can also be firm.) Instead of focusing on punishment, though, we prioritized education and support.

We added modules to our web training to help content creators understand how screen readers interpret emails and websites. We hosted hands-on demonstrations, showing how inaccessible practices could exclude people and create unnecessary barriers. Watching my colleagues connect the dots during these sessions was rewarding. They weren't resistant—they just didn't realize the impact of their choices.

The work didn't stop with email. Our videographer teamed up with an intern to add closed captions to our back catalog of marketing videos. We developed guidelines for adding alt-text to web images and made accessibility training a standard part of our web content management curriculum. We even created Braille signs for our wayfinding kiosks. What began as a response to one problem turned into a cultural shift. Accessibility became central to how we communicated as a campus.

Accessibility is About Human Beings

Imagine you're a student excited about applying to college. You pull up the website, eager to learn more—only to find that none of the links work with your screen reader. The application page? Unreadable. The scholarship info? Inaccessible. The message? You don't belong here. Not because the university said so, but because they never considered you in the first place.

Or imagine a parent who is hard of hearing trying to follow a virtual campus tour without captions. That parent isn't just missing information; they're losing the chance to feel connected to your campus. These aren't minor inconveniences. They're barriers. And those barriers can make higher education feel out of reach.

Here's a number that might surprise you: one in five college students has a disability. One in five. Let that sink in. Accessibility isn't a niche issue affecting a tiny fraction of your audience. It's a reality for a considerable part of the student population. And if we're serious about serving students, we must make our institutions accessible to them.

Imagine a student with a physical disability arriving on your campus. Ramps are where they should be, elevators work reliably, and automatic doors open easily. Signs are clear and easy to understand. What does that say? It says,

"You belong here. We've thought about your needs. You can thrive here."

Or think of a prospective student navigating your website. They find a dedicated page for learning accommodations written in plain, approachable language. There are step-by-step guides that make it simple to understand how to access services. And there are guides that walk through the process in multiple formats to address multiple learning styles. That's your institution saying, "We care about you."

Marketers cannot view accessibility as a tech problem to hand off to IT or the disability services office. It's a human issue that requires recognizing the obstacles others face—obstacles we might overlook ourselves—and asking, "How can we make this easier for someone else?" Sometimes, that means simplifying a webpage. Sometimes, it's adding captions to videos or using clear, straightforward language. The fixes aren't always complicated, but they can make a difference.

Accessibility goes beyond compliance. It speaks to credibility. If your website talks about diversity but locks out students who use screen readers, what message are you really sending? If your university claims to be student-centered but forgets to caption videos, how student-centered are you really? Students and families notice these gaps. And when they do, they see a broken promise.

The good news is that accessible design isn't just for people with disabilities. That tiny, unreadable font? The hard-to-navigate website? The video without captions? Those things frustrate *everyone*. When you design for accessibility, you create a better experience for all users, whether on they are on their laptop at home, using a smartphone on the go, or trying to read your website late at night on a dim screen.

When a student can easily find what they're looking for, when a parent feels welcomed and informed, that builds trust.

You don't have to be perfect. You do have to show effort that demonstrates that you care enough to try.

Lead by Example

Accessibility starts at the top. When campus leaders champion accessibility, it transforms the campus mentality from a "should do" into a "must do."

Take leadership communications. Every presidential email, social post, or town hall presentation is a statement about your values. Clear fonts that everyone can read. Alt text that brings images to life for screen readers. Sign language interpreters at every event. Video captions that open conversations to all. When leaders embrace these practices, they show that inclusion matters in everything we do.

Leadership also needs to celebrate success. Launching a more accessible website, improving campus pathways, and creating easier-to-read campus signage deserve as much attention as a winning football team or a Fulbright Scholar. When leaders recognize these milestones, they also celebrate the collective work it took to achieve them and inspire others to join the journey.

Accessibility needs to be woven into strategic plans and discussed at board meetings. When leaders keep accessibility at the forefront, it becomes part of the institutional DNA rather than just another initiative.

This commitment from the top creates a ripple effect. It transforms accessibility from a compliance issue into a shared value that defines your community.

Building Accessible Websites

Your website is the central hub for your institution's digital presence. It's where prospective students explore programs, parents investigate financial aid, and alumni check out campus events. For all these audiences, accessibility starts with thoughtful design and consistent maintenance.

Accessible websites use tools like alt-text, which allows screen readers to describe images to visually impaired users. Keyboard navigation ensures that people who can't use a mouse can still move through your site seamlessly. High-contrast designs and large, readable fonts make content easier to consume for everyone, including those with low vision or color blindness.

Creating and maintaining an accessible website is an ongoing process. Regular audits using WAVE or Axe can help you catch and correct barriers. Incorporating user feedback, especially from people with disabilities, gives you real-world insights into what's working and what's not. Accessibility isn't something you "complete" once; it's a continuous commitment.

Crafting Inclusive Social Media

Social media is where your institution's personality comes to life. It's where prospective students get their first taste of campus culture, where current students find community, and where alumni stay connected to the place that helped shape their story. But with that incredible power to engage comes an important responsibility: ensuring everyone can participate in the conversation.

- Video captions are an essential starting point, not only for users who are deaf or hard of hearing but for anyone scrolling through their feed in a quiet or noisy space.
- Alt-text for images is equally important. Platforms like Instagram, Bluesky, and Facebook allow you to add text descriptions to images, making them accessible to people who rely on screen readers. On Bluesky, you can adjust your settings to make posting an image without entering alt-text impossible.
- Avoid dense graphics overloaded with text, as these can be difficult to interpret both visually and with assistive technologies. Instead, convey essential information in captions or accompanying posts.

Staying current with platform-specific accessibility features, like Instagram's accessibility tags or Bluesky's image description tools, keeps your social media presence inclusive. These small adjustments make a big difference in ensuring everyone can connect with your content.

Designing Accessible Emails

Email is a cornerstone of higher education marketing, but accessibility is often overlooked in this channel. Designing an email that everyone can read and interact with begins with structure and simplicity.

- Start with a logical layout. Use headings to organize content and make navigation easier for screen readers.

- Choose readable fonts—nothing overly decorative—and ensure that text is large enough to read comfortably.
- Links and buttons should be descriptive, so instead of "Click here," use text like "Explore housing options" or "Learn more about financial aid." This clarity helps everyone, not just those using assistive technologies.
- Pay attention to visual elements. Image-heavy designs may look appealing but can pose challenges if the images contain critical text.
- Always include alt text for images and ensure any essential information is available in plain text within the email body.
- Use clear contrast and avoid relying solely on color to highlight links or buttons. Remember, accessibility is about functionality, not just aesthetics.

Make Accessibility a Team Effort

Creating a culture of accessibility takes collaboration, education, and a shared commitment to inclusion. Accessibility isn't something one person or one team can handle alone. It's a collective responsibility that needs to be embedded across your institution.

Start by offering regular accessibility training for faculty, staff, and marketing teams. Many people simply don't know what goes into making content accessible, and that's okay—it's our job to help them learn. Whether it's understanding how to write effective alt-text, choosing readable fonts, or using color contrast tools, these skills are essential for anyone creating or sharing content. Accessibility training improves outcomes and builds awareness, helping your community see why this work matters.

Another way to prioritize accessibility is by involving students, faculty, and community members with disabilities when developing strategies or testing content. Their lived experiences offer invaluable insights. By including these voices, you're not only improving the accessibility of your content but also demonstrating a genuine commitment to inclusion.

Finally, accessibility advocates within departments should be appointed to champion this work. These advocates can serve as go-to resources, providing guidance and support when questions arise. They don't need to be experts on every aspect of accessibility, but they can help keep accessibility in mind and encourage their teams to adopt best practices. This leadership ensures that accessibility becomes a shared priority, not a task for the marketing team or IT department.

Build Accessibility Benchmarks into KPIs: Turning Intentions into Action

Embedding accessibility into your KPIs sends a message. It says, "Inclusion isn't optional here; it's who we are." By making accessibility a standard for success, you create accountability and foster a culture that prioritizes equitable experiences for everyone. That's how you turn words into action and make accessibility a non-negotiable part of your marketing vision.

Make Accessibility Measurable

Accessibility-specific KPIs should reflect quantitative and qualitative measures to capture the full scope of your efforts. For example, you might track metrics like:

- **Percentage of Digital Assets Captioned:** This includes ensuring that every video, from social media snippets to full-length webinars, is captioned accurately.
- **Alt Text Accuracy Rates:** Instead of merely checking whether alt text exists, evaluate how well it describes the content. Effective alt text should be meaningful descriptors for users relying on screen readers.
- **Website Accessibility Scores:** Use tools like WAVE, Siteimprove, or Axe to assess your website's accessibility, aiming for improvements over time.
- **Feedback from Users with Disabilities:** Regularly survey or interview stakeholders with disabilities to understand their experiences with your digital assets and overall communication.

Transparency and Accountability

Publicly sharing your accessibility goals and progress adds a layer of accountability that pushes your institution to stay on track. This could take the form of:

- **Annual Accessibility Reports:** Publish a summary of your achievements, challenges, and areas for growth. Include metrics like the

number of videos captioned, updates to website accessibility, or feedback collected from users with disabilities.
- **Real-Time Dashboards:** Create an internal or external dashboard that tracks progress toward accessibility goals. Transparency fosters trust, both within your team and among your audience.
- **Accessibility Recognition:** Share success stories about how your accessibility efforts have positively impacted students, parents, or community members. For example, feature a student who found it easier to navigate your website or a parent who appreciated the captions on a virtual tour.

Tying Accessibility to Broader Success Metrics

Accessibility isn't just a moral or legal imperative – it's also a strategic advantage that drives better engagement and broader reach. When digital assets are more accessible, they're often more usable for everyone.

- **Improved SEO:** Captioned videos and descriptive alt text enhance search engine optimization, making your content more discoverable.
- **Increased Engagement:** Accessible content removes barriers, enabling a broader audience to interact with and share your materials.
- **Enhanced Reputation:** Demonstrating a commitment to inclusion reflects your institution's brand positively and attracts

students and families who value diversity and equity.

♥

Insights and Impact Plan

Hype-Free Insights

- **Accessibility is About Inclusion, Not Just Compliance:** Accessibility goes beyond legal standards. It fosters an inclusive culture that ensures everyone feels valued and welcome.

- **Transforming Perceptions and Building Trust**: Accessible practices, like captioned videos, user-friendly websites, and inclusive campus communications, demonstrate care and empathy. These efforts build trust and create meaningful connections that resonate long-term.
- **Accessibility Benefits Everyone:** Improvements like better navigation, clear communication, and user-friendly digital platforms don't just help individuals with disabilities—they enhance the user experience, increasing engagement and usability.
- **Leadership as a Catalyst:** Institutional leaders are critical in prioritizing accessibility. Their advocacy sets the tone, inspires others, and integrates accessibility into the fabric of strategic goals.
- **Accessibility as a Strategic Advantage:** Inclusive design, seamless navigation, and

accessible content are powerful differentiators, making institutions more appealing to prospective students and families.

Impact Plan

- **Start with Education:** Offer regular accessibility training for faculty and staff to raise awareness and build essential skills.
- **Involve Stakeholders:** Engage students, faculty, and community members with disabilities in developing strategies or testing content to ensure real-world applicability.
- **Review Your Digital Accessibility:** Use tools like alt-text, keyboard navigation, and high-contrast designs to ensure accessibility for users with visual, auditory, and physical disabilities. Caption all videos and use alt-text for all images.
- **Assess Your Physical Accessibility:** Ensure campus navigation is seamless, with reliable elevators, accessible ramps, and clear signage. Highlight accessible features in campus tours and other marketing materials.
- **Set Accessibility KPIs:** Track metrics like the percentage of captioned videos, alt-text accuracy rates, and website accessibility scores.

Chapter 9
Empathy-Driven Marketing Exercises

Empathy isn't theoretical. It's practical and has to show up in how you work. That's where these exercises come in. They're your chance to get out of your head, step into someone else's shoes (even if they're metaphorical), and rethink how you communicate.

If you want your marketing to connect with people, you need to see the world through their eyes. You must move past "What do we want to say?" and dive into "What do they need to hear?" These exercises aren't just for fun (though they can be); they are designed to help you and your team get honest about the humans on the other end of your campaigns.

We all fall into ruts. We default to our own perspectives and forget what it's like to be the overwhelmed high school junior, the stressed-out parent, or the alumnus debating whether to answer that fundraising call. These exercises shake that up. They'll help you challenge assumptions, uncover blind spots, and spark ideas you might never have considered otherwise.

Some exercises will ask you to role-play (don't worry, no costumes required). Others will push you to dissect your current messaging and see it with fresh eyes. All of them are designed to help you build strategies that aren't just about what you want to say but about what your audience needs to feel.

You don't need to tackle them all at once. Pick one. Try it. See what happens. You might be surprised by what you learn about your audience and your own team's perspective.

Persona Storytelling Exercise

Persona storytelling workshops help your team *feel* what it's like to be in your audience's shoes. That emotional connection translates into authentic and effective campaigns. When you approach your audience with this level of empathy, you're building trust and fostering belonging.

Objective: Help teams truly see their audience—not as data points or demographic segments but as real people with complex lives, goals, and emotions. Numbers can tell you *who* your audience is, but stories help you understand *their feelings and needs*.

How It Works:

Step 1: Set the Stage: Begin with a short introduction to explain the workshop's purpose. Emphasize that the goal is to step into your audience's shoes and explore their challenges and motivations. Avoiding unconscious biases and approaching the exercise with fresh, clear eyes is important.

Step 2: Divide and Assign Personas: Split the team into small groups of 3-5 people. Assign each group a specific audience persona. Each persona should have a basic description, including demographic details, key challenges, and high-level goals. For example:

- **First-Generation College Student:** Navigating the overwhelming process of applications, worried about affordability, and unsure if they'll belong.
- **Working Parent Considering an Online Degree:** Balancing work, kids, and aspirations for career advancement, but skeptical about fitting coursework into an already packed schedule.
- **Alumnus Reconnecting with the Institution:** Curious about ways to get involved but unsure if the university still feels relevant to their current life.

Step 3: Flesh Out the Persona: Give the groups time to "fill in the blanks." Encourage them to get creative, imagining specifics like:

- A typical day in their persona's life.
- Pain points they might encounter (e.g., confusion over financial aid, difficulty finding flexible class schedules, or feelings of isolation).
- Emotional drivers include hope, fear, pride, and belonging.

Step 4: Craft a "Day in the Life" Narrative: Have each group build a short story around their persona's experience. These narratives help the team see the human side of their audience personas, including the obstacles and emotions they face. For example:

- **Morning:** A working parent drops their kids off at school, thinking about how an online degree could help them land a promotion.
- **Afternoon:** They try to carve out time to research programs but feel overwhelmed by jargon and unclear requirements on university websites.
- **Evening:** They sit down with their spouse to discuss the investment and wonder if they're too old to return to school.

Step 5: Share and Reflect as a Team: Bring everyone together to share their persona's story. As each group presents, encourage the rest of the team to note common themes and insights. Facilitate a discussion around:

- What stood out about the persona's experience?
- Which pain points could your institution address?
- What emotional needs should your campaigns or support initiatives focus on?
- What unconscious biases or institutional assumptions might be impacting the persona's journey?

Step 6: Identify Actionable Takeaways: Wrap up by translating insights into action. For example:

- Messaging tweaks to address specific fears or aspirations.
- Improvements to digital experiences, like clearer navigation for first-generation students.
- New support initiatives, such as flexible advising hours for working parents.

Empathy Mapping Exercise

Empathy mapping helps teams see their audience's journey's emotional and practical realities. When you understand what your audience is thinking, feeling, doing, and hearing, you can create strategies that connect.

Objective: Bring your audience's experience to life by visualizing their thoughts, feelings, actions, and influences. This exercise helps teams step out of their perspectives and into the shoes of the people they're trying to reach. When you can clearly see their needs, you can create experiences that genuinely resonate. It's important for your team to not solely base this work on their own personal experiences. Stress that they consider other perspectives as well and allow everyone to share their points of view.

How It Works:

Step 1: Prepare the Framework: Start with a large sheet of paper, a whiteboard, or a digital collaboration tool. Divide it into four quadrants and label them:

- **Thinking**: What's going through their minds? What are their hopes, fears, and concerns?
- **Feeling**: What emotions are they experiencing? Excitement? Frustration? Anxiety?
- **Doing**: What actions are they taking? What's their behavior during this process?
- **Hearing**: What external messages or influences are shaping their perceptions? This could include peer feedback, social media chatter, or marketing campaigns.

Step 2: Select an Audience: Choose a specific audience to focus on. For example:

- Prospective students visiting your website.
- Parents attending an open house.
- Alumni considering whether to donate.

Step 3: Set the Scene: Imagine a scenario where this audience interacts with your institution. For example, a prospective student exploring your website for the first time. Think about their mindset, goals, and challenges as they navigate this experience.

Step 4: Brainstorm in Teams: Gather your team and start filling each quadrant with ideas. Keep the conversation flowing and encourage creativity. Here's how to think about each section:

- **Thinking**: What are they questioning?

- **Feeling**: How do they feel during this process?
- **Doing**: What actions are they taking?
- **Hearing**: What's influencing them?

Step 5: Fill in the Gaps: Once you've brainstormed, step back and look for gaps. Are there any important aspects of the experience you've missed? For example:

- Have you considered external stressors like deadlines or family expectations?
- Are you addressing their unspoken fears or doubts?

Step 6: Reflect and Adjust: Review the completed map as a team and ask:

- Does our current strategy address these thoughts, feelings, actions, and influences?
- Are we unintentionally adding to their stress or confusion?
- How can we better align our messaging, processes, or support to meet their needs?

Step 7: Create Actionable Insights: Use the empathy map as a springboard for improvements. For example:

- If prospective students feel overwhelmed by a complicated application process, simplify your website navigation and add clear, step-by-step guides.

- If they hear mixed messages about affordability, create content that explains financial aid in relatable, transparent language.

Accessibility Walkthrough Exercise

An accessibility walkthrough doesn't just highlight technical fixes—it creates empathy. Team members see firsthand what it feels like to face barriers, making the issue personal. That's often the spark needed to drive meaningful change.

When you address accessibility gaps you're creating a better experience for everyone. Features like captions, simplified navigation, and faster load times benefit all users, regardless of their circumstances.

Objective: Step into the shoes of individuals with diverse needs to identify and address barriers that could prevent them from fully engaging with your website, materials, or campus. This walkthrough helps uncover those barriers so you can fix them and create a more welcoming environment.

How It Works

Step 1: Set the Stage: Bring together a group of team members for the exercise. This isn't just for admissions or marketing—it's for anyone involved in shaping the user experience, from housing to facilities management. Frame the walkthrough as an opportunity to identify barriers and opportunities for improvement, not a blame game.

Step 2: Assign Roles: To make the experience immersive and impactful, assign team members personas or scenarios to explore. Examples include:

- **Visually Impaired User**: Use a screen reader or simulate low vision by reducing screen brightness or using grayscale filters.
- **Mobility-Impaired Visitor**: Imagine navigating campus in a wheelchair, noting ramp placements, door widths, and elevator functionality. (Bonus if you can find a wheelchair to borrow.)
- **Non-Native English Speaker**: Access materials or websites to assess readability and the availability of translations or clear language.
- **User with Slow Internet**: Simulate slow connections to understand how long it takes for pages to load or if critical content fails to appear.

Step 3: Conduct the Walkthrough: Have team members explore your website, materials, or campus using the lens of their assigned role. For example:

- Visiting key webpages (e.g., application, financial aid, or virtual tour).
- Attempting to complete a task, like filling out an application, registering for an event, or finding a specific office on campus.
- Reviewing materials like brochures or event schedules for clarity and accessibility.

- Walking or wheeling the physical campus to evaluate pathways, building entrances, and signage.

Step 4: Document the Experience: As participants move through their tasks, ask them to jot down notes on barriers they encounter. Examples include:

- "The screen reader skips critical navigation links on the financial aid page."
- "The admissions page took over 10 seconds to load on a simulated slow connection."
- "Campus map signage doesn't include Braille or tactile features for visually impaired visitors."
- "This form uses academic jargon that might confuse someone new to higher education."

Step 5: Debrief as a Team: Come back together to discuss findings. Encourage participants to share what surprised or frustrated them during the exercise. Highlight any patterns or recurring issues that emerged across roles.

Step 6: Create an Action Plan: Use the insights gathered to prioritize accessibility improvements. Examples of actionable steps include:

- Adding alt-text to all images and ensuring screen readers can navigate forms.
- Optimizing the website for slower internet speeds or mobile devices.

- Including translations or plain-language summaries for complex documents.
- Installing automatic doors, tactile signage, or additional ramps on campus.

Empathy Audit

If your communications feel like they're falling flat—failing to spark interest or leaving your audience unengaged—it's time to take a step back and reevaluate. An empathy audit helps you uncover blind spots, refine your tone, and ensure you're connecting on a human level.

Objective: To evaluate whether your existing communications show a genuine understanding of your audience's needs, emotions, and perspectives and to identify opportunities to make your messaging more authentic, inclusive, and impactful.

How It Works

Step 1: Gather Examples: Start by collecting a range of recent communications like emails, social media posts, ad campaigns, brochures, or website content. Aim for a mix of formats and topics, from marketing materials to event invites or transactional messages.

Step 2: Assemble the Team: Include a diverse group of stakeholders in the process, such as marketing staff, student services reps, admissions counselors, and even students or alumni. Different perspectives will help uncover blind spots.

Step 3: Set the Lens: Establish the mindset for the audit. The focus isn't to critique for the sake of nitpicking but to evaluate whether the message truly reflects empathy and understanding. Keep these guiding principles in mind:

- **Audience-First:** Are we speaking to their concerns, hopes, or challenges?
- **Tone:** Does this feel human, inclusive, and authentic?
- **Barriers:** Are there assumptions or unintentional exclusions that could alienate someone?

Step 4: Review Each Piece with Key Questions: Does this align with the audience's emotional state or priorities? Think about what your audience might feel when engaging with this content. For instance:

- Are prospective students excited but nervous?
- Are parents seeking reassurance about finances or safety?
- Is the tone aligned with their mindset?
- If your message doesn't address what's on their minds, it's a missed opportunity to connect.

Step 5: Are there unintentional barriers or assumptions? Look for anything that might exclude or alienate someone. Examples include:

- Jargon that's confusing to first-generation students.

- Images that lack diversity or fail to represent the intended audience.
- Instructions or links that don't work well on mobile devices.
- Language that assumes the reader already knows specific steps or terms.

Step 6: Does the tone feel authentic, caring, and inclusive? Audit the tone of voice:

- Is it warm and approachable, or does it feel cold and robotic?
- Does it celebrate and empower the audience, or does it feel condescending?
- Are you using inclusive language that resonates across diverse audiences?

Step 7: Document Findings: As you evaluate, take detailed notes on each piece. Highlight areas where the communication succeeds and where it falls short. For example:

- "The tone is friendly, but it assumes everyone knows how FAFSA works. Consider linking to a beginner's guide."
- "This social media post celebrates campus diversity, but the photo doesn't reflect that diversity."
- "The message addresses cost concerns but misses the opportunity to acknowledge how financial aid supports families."

Step 8: Discuss as a Team: Bring the group together to share insights. Encourage an open dialogue about what worked, what didn't, and why. Use this time to brainstorm solutions for improving tone, language, or presentation.

Step 9: Create an Action Plan: Use your findings to develop recommendations for improving the content and your overall communication strategy. For example:

- Adjust tone guidelines to ensure warmth and inclusivity.
- Update visuals to better reflect the diversity of your audience.
- Simplify processes and provide clear instructions to reduce barriers.

Role-Reversal Exercise

This exercise highlights not only what you're saying but how it's being received. That shift—from your perspective to theirs—can transform your messaging into something that truly resonates and builds trust.

Objective: Shift the focus from what *you* want to communicate to what *your audience* feels, needs, and values by stepping into their shoes. By thinking like your audience, you'll uncover what truly resonates—and avoid the missteps that make them tune out.

How It Works:

Step 1: Set the Stage: Gather your team and assign each person a specific audience persona. Examples could include:

- A first-generation high school senior feeling overwhelmed by the college search process.
- A working parent juggling multiple responsibilities while considering an online degree.
- A skeptical alumna who hasn't engaged with your institution since graduation.

Step 2: Provide some quick background on each persona, including their goals (i.e., getting a good job after graduation, having the full college experience, making friends), challenges (i.e., financial barriers, first-generation status), and drivers.

Step 3: Present the Scenario: Share a common marketing scenario your audience might encounter, such as:

- Receiving a financial aid email with an unfamiliar process.
- Exploring a virtual tour for the first time.
- Seeing a recruitment ad pop up on social media.
- Reading through an alumni giving appeal.

Step 4: Persona Responses: Ask each team member to respond *as their assigned persona*. Encourage them to think about:

- **Feelings:** What emotions does this communication spark? Excitement? Confusion? Frustration? Relief?
- **Needs:** What questions or concerns do they have at this moment? Is this message answering them?
- **Reactions:** Would they engage further (click, respond, or share), or would they dismiss it? Why?

Step 5: Document Insights: Capture responses from each persona. What surprised you? Where did your messaging flounder? What aspects of the communication stood out as positive or helpful?

Step 6: Refine and Adjust: Use these insights to refine your strategies. Maybe the financial aid email needs more straightforward language and a clear call-to-action. Perhaps the virtual tour would benefit from a more personal tone or captions for inclusivity. Or maybe the alumni giving appeal would resonate better if it celebrated specific alumni stories instead of just asking for money.

Aligning Campaign Timing with Audience Rhythms

When it comes to marketing and communication, we often focus on *what* to say. But just as important is *when* to say it. Understanding your audience means considering their mindset. What's happening in their lives? What are they juggling? And are you showing up at the right moment to add value, or the wrong one, creating frustration?

This exercise is designed to help you rethink your approach to timing. By the end of this exercise, you'll have a clearer picture of your audience's timing needs and actionable strategies to meet them where they are.

Objective: To understand your audience's life rhythms and key events throughout the year, identify misalignments between your current communication schedule and your audience's calendar, and create a timing strategy that aligns messaging with moments when your audience is most receptive.

How It Works

Step 1: Understand Your Audience's Calendar: Break into small groups or work individually to create a timeline of your audience's year. Use research, focus group feedback, or staff insights to fill in key events. For traditional students, map out academic milestones (e.g., finals, application deadlines, graduation prep). For adult learners, highlight major personal or seasonal events (e.g., back-to-school time, tax season, New Year).

Step 2: Overlay Your Communication Calendar: Compare your communication schedule with your audience's calendar to identify conflicts or missed opportunities. Use a second layer (transparent sheet or digital overlay) to place your current campaigns on the audience's calendar. Look for campaigns timed during busy or distracted periods and key times when no campaigns are running, but your audience may be receptive.

Step 3: Refine Your Timing Strategy: Highlight campaigns that need timing adjustments. Brainstorm opportunities for new campaigns during high-impact moments (e.g., post-New Year's for adult learners).

Step 4: Run a Pilot Test: Identify one or two campaigns to reschedule based on your refined timing strategy. Run A/B tests to compare engagement rates (e.g., email opens, clicks, or conversions).

Step 5: Debrief:

- What were the most surprising timing conflicts or gaps you discovered?
- How do these timing adjustments show empathy for your audience?
- How can you incorporate timing insights into future campaign planning?

Chapter 10
Creating Environments Where People (and Ideas) Thrive

If your team doesn't feel cared for, how can they create campaigns that genuinely connect? Empathy-driven marketing starts from within. If leadership doesn't model empathy daily, don't expect it to show up in your branding, messaging, or culture.

Culture is a mirror of leadership. If you're the kind of leader who treats people with respect and understanding, your team is far more likely to reflect that in how they approach their work. This leadership lays the groundwork for authentic, impactful campaigns, especially in marketing, where understanding the audience's needs is everything.

Empathy-driven leaders also create spaces where team members feel safe to speak up. That safety matters. When people trust their voices will be heard (and respected), they're much more likely to share honest feedback and ideas. A team that feels seen and valued is far more willing to approach their work with genuine care.

Leading with empathy shapes the DNA of your team. When you live the values you want reflected in your marketing, those values become second nature. They infuse everything your team does, from brainstorming campaigns to crafting student interactions. That's how you create marketing that embodies genuine empathy.

Psychological Safety Allows Wild Ideas to Flourish

"What if we had something more like a town hall that was a little ... flashier? Kind of like a TedTalk?"

I vividly recall posing that question in my first few months as chief marketing officer at Winston-Salem State University. Chancellor Elwood Robinson had pulled together a group of "creative thinkers" to help brainstorm how to roll out our new strategic plan. After I asked that, I locked eyes with one of the university's deans, Corey Walker. I could tell he was excited by it, too. Over the next ten minutes, we riffed off each other until that spark of an idea became wild and untamable.

Rather than have Chancellor Robinson stand behind a podium and give a speech about the audacious strategic plan the campus had just built, we did something much more "on brand" for WSSU. More than a third of the campus community showed up for an event that featured the marching band, cheerleaders, and TedTalk-style speeches from leadership, students, alumni, and community members.

People were on their feet, cheering and dancing to the fight song. Thunderous standing ovations followed the inspiring speeches. The campus was *abuzz* with people talking about their excitement about the direction the university was headed.

Imagine that—a third of your campus willingly attending a strategic plan rollout! People having FOMO over missing *speeches!* People actually *excited* about implementing the strategic plan!

This wild idea was only possible because Chancellor Robinson had created the psychological safety needed for Corey and me—and many others—to throw out off-the-wall suggestions without fear of judgment or eye-rolls.

The greatest ideas never get spoken in toxic cultures. Without psychological safety, your best thinkers stay silent. And when people stay silent, innovation dies.

We've all been there: sitting in a meeting, that spark of an idea flickering to life, and then... silence. Your heart races. Your palms get sweaty. You start mentally talking yourself out of speaking up.

Why? Because workplace cultures can be brutal. One wrong word, one slightly off-pitch suggestion, and suddenly, you're branded as someone who doesn't get it. Sharing an idea—especially an out-of-the-box one—can feel like walking a tightrope. And without psychological safety, those ideas can end up bottled up.

Imagine a workplace where ideas don't feel like risks. Where speaking up doesn't feel like stepping onto a tightrope. Where curiosity matters more than looking smart. That's what psychological safety makes possible. What if you knew your leadership had your back and, even if the idea is terrible, your colleagues would listen and find the nuggets that are worthy of further consideration?

Leaders have the power to create that type of environment. Let me rephrase that: Leaders have an *obligation* to create that kind of environment. You are missing out if your team doesn't feel comfortable speaking up or sharing ideas.

Leadership doesn't mean having all the answers. It means creating space for your team to find them together. Think about the last time you felt truly comfortable speaking up in a meeting, sharing a half-formed idea, or admitting you were stuck. That is what psychological safety feels like.

When people genuinely fear being shot down or embarrassed, they shut down. They stop offering ideas. They play it safe. But when a leader creates an environment where vulnerability isn't weakness—where mistakes are seen as learning opportunities —people start taking smart risks. They speak up. They collaborate with energy that can't be forced or faked.

Whenever I talk about leading with empathy, people always ask me, "But what about accountability?" This points to a fundamental misunderstanding of what empathy is. Empathy doesn't equal "being nice." When mistakes are made, feedback is necessary, but it needs to be delivered with kindness. When someone drops the ball, they need to be called out, but not in packed meetings in front of others. When performance slips, it needs to be addressed, but not without trying to understand if something deeper is happening.

Psychological safety isn't letting people say or do anything without consequences—it's fostering a space where they feel safe to be authentic. Where an "imperfect" or wild idea isn't a career-ending mistake but a potential breakthrough waiting to be shaped. Where curiosity matters more than looking smart.

When people feel truly safe, they start showing up differently. They bring their whole selves to work. They're willing to take calculated risks, challenge assumptions, and admit what they don't know. That vulnerability is not weakness. It's the foundation of genuine innovation.

Trust isn't something you mandate. It's something you build, conversation by conversation, gesture by gesture. When you do, your team becomes more than a group of individuals. They become a living, breathing organism capable of weathering any storm.

How to Foster Psychological Safety

Most workplaces are where good ideas go to die. Endless meetings that go nowhere. People keeping quiet because they've learned it's safer to just nod along. It doesn't have to be this way. What if your workplace became a space where people *wanted* to speak up and share their wildest, most groundbreaking ideas? It's possible if you are intentional. And it starts with you.

Being approachable isn't as simple as saying, "My door is always open." (How often does that actually get used?) It's means showing up differently. Being human. When someone's talking to you, put down your phone. Make eye contact. Act like you actually care—because you should. If someone shares a concern, don't rush to defend the status quo or fix it immediately. Instead, get curious. Ask them, "What's not working?" or "How do you see this playing out?" Show them that you're there to understand—not just respond.

And words matter. The difference between "We've tried that before" and "That's an interesting idea—tell me more about how you see it working" is night and day. One shuts the door; the other cracks it open. That second response says, "I'm willing to reconsider." It shows you're open to revisiting old ideas or trying something new.

Leaders need to focus on creating space where honest conversations can happen. Where ideas can percolate. And no, not every conversation needs a formal meeting with an agenda. Maybe it's a weekly coffee chat where the whole team shares ideas. Perhaps it's a Slack channel where people can share their wildest suggestions without judgment. It could even be as simple as starting your one-on-ones with, "What's something you've been thinking about lately that we haven't talked about yet?" The format doesn't matter nearly as much as the intention. Give people permission to speak—and make it clear you're actually listening.

You're trying to foster a workplace where people can show up fully—messy ideas, half-baked thoughts, bold suggestions, and all. When people feel safe enough to bring their whole selves to work, things start to really cook. Innovation. Engagement. Growth.

If you're not creating that space, you're missing out. Because the quieter your team gets, the more you're losing —perspectives, creativity, and solutions you might not have even considered.

Avoid New Manager Syndrome

Taking on a new leadership role is exciting, but it can also come with challenges—especially if you fall into the trap of "new manager syndrome." This common pitfall occurs when new leaders, eager to make their mark, act too quickly or misstep in ways that undermine trust and morale.

Jumping in with sweeping changes before understanding the organization's dynamics can backfire. Instead, prioritize listening. Meet with your team and stakeholders to understand their perspectives. Ask thoughtful questions like, What's working well here? What are the most significant pain points? What's one thing you wish could change?

It's natural to want to make improvements, but overhauling processes or restructuring too quickly can alienate your team. Before implementing changes, assess whether they are necessary and align with the organization's goals. Start small—build momentum with quick wins, demonstrating your ability to enhance what's already in place without disrupting what works.

It's tempting to feel like you need to save the day or prove your value by solving every problem. But true leadership empowers others. Delegate effectively, trust your team's expertise, and collaborate to find solutions. Recognize that your role is to guide, not micromanage.

Defeat Imposter Syndrome

Imposter syndrome whispers to even the most accomplished professionals, "You're not enough," driving them to overcompensate in ways that detract from their full potential and hold them back as leaders. When they own their expertise, they liberate themselves from the relentless need to prove their worth.

Professionals who embrace their accomplishments and unique value shed the paralyzing self-doubt that comes with imposter syndrome. Rather than being consumed by the fear of inadequacy or the pressure to constantly validate themselves, they approach their work with quiet confidence. They stop second-guessing every decision and start trusting their instincts and experience.

When you stop trying to prove you belong in the room, you become free to fully participate in the conversation. This shift allows you to listen more deeply, something essential for effective leadership and collaboration.

Owning your expertise creates space for empathy. Instead of focusing inward on insecurities, you can direct your attention outward. You begin to see conversations not as performance reviews but as opportunities for connection and understanding.

This mindset frees you from the destructive perfectionism that often accompanies self-doubt and allows you to focus on what matters most: the task at hand and the people you serve.

Model Vulnerability

Leadership comes with a ridiculous amount of pressure. And there seems to be an unwritten rulebook that says you've got to be bulletproof. Always confident. Never rattled. Always with the perfect answer tucked in your back pocket.

That's complete garbage.

The most influential leaders I've ever worked with weren't the ones who pretended to be superhuman. They were brave enough to say, "I don't know," or "I'm struggling with this." The ones who could look a team in the eye and admit when they were uncertain. Real leadership looks messy. It looks like saying, "I messed up" and actually meaning it. Not the non-apology where you're basically just sorry you got caught, but a genuine, "I didn't get this right, and here's what I'm learning." Nobody wants to work for a robot. Those leaders who act like they've never screwed up? They're not impressive. They're just exhausting. (Been there, done that, got the T-shirt.)

When a project tanks, don't hide or blame it on someone else. Step up. Say something like, "That didn't go how I expected. What can we learn from this?" That's not weakness. That's strength. That shows your team you're more interested in growing than looking perfect.

Communication breaking down? Own it. "I didn't

explain this clearly, and that's on me." Simple. Direct. No excuses.

And please stop pretending you know everything. What are the most powerful words a leader can say? "I'm not sure. What are your thoughts?" or "I'm not sure what the best approach is here, but I trust this team's expertise. Let's brainstorm together." It turns out people don't want a know-it-all. (We really, really don't.) They want someone willing to learn alongside them. Share your actual stories. The times you failed. The risks that didn't pay off. Not some sanitized LinkedIn humble-brag, but real, raw moments of learning. That's how you become human to your team.

Real leaders create environments where people feel safe exploring those answers. Where mistakes are just another step in the learning process. Where being authentic matters more than looking invincible.

Vulnerability isn't a sign of weakness—it's a commitment to growth. Always. And when you have the courage to be real, you create space for others to do the same.

Acknowledge and Validate Emotions

Most leaders are terrible at handling emotions. When someone's struggling, the knee-jerk response is often to shut it down. "Toughen up." "Breathe. It's not that bad." "It just is what it is."

But emotions aren't a problem that needs to be fixed. They're signals to be heard.

When someone on your team is frustrated, they're not looking for you to wave a magic wand and make everything perfect. They want to know that what they're feeling makes sense. That you actually see them and hear them.

Imagine your team member comes to you stressed about a project. The wrong move? Immediately jumping into problem-solving mode. The right move? First, just listen. "This sounds really tough. Walk me through what you're experiencing."

Validation isn't agreeing with everything—it's demonstrating understanding. Saying, "I can see why this feels overwhelming; let's find a solution together," builds trust far more than a dismissive "Don't worry about it" or "I'll handle it."

The goal isn't to eliminate their feelings. The goal is to create a space where feelings are welcome. Where people know they can be human at work without being judged.

People don't leave jobs. They leave environments where they don't feel heard.

Create Clear Expectations

Psychological safety isn't a free pass. You can't just let everything slide or avoid tough conversations. You have to create an environment where accountability actually means something.

Think about the worst workplace you've ever been in. Chances are, the rules were either totally random or completely inconsistent. Some people got away with murder, while others were crucified for tiny mistakes. That's not accountability. That's chaos.

Real accountability looks like clarity. No hidden rules. No moving goalposts. Everyone knows what's expected and what happens if those expectations aren't met. It's like a team playbook where everyone can see the rules. When you promise something to your team—whether it's looking into their workload, fighting for their resources, or giving honest feedback—you've got to follow through. And if something's taking longer than expected? Don't ghost them. Keep them in the loop.

"Hey, I'm still working on those workload concerns. It's taking longer than I hoped, but I haven't forgotten" makes a huge difference. It says, "You matter. Your concerns matter."

Accountability creates systems where people know they will be treated fairly. Where the rules make sense. Where everyone— including you—is playing by the same playbook.

Celebrate Contributions and Lessons Learned

Recognizing effort isn't the same as giving out participation trophies. It means honoring the person behind the work. When someone pours their energy and creativity into a project—whether it soars or stumbles—that deserves recognition. Failure isn't the enemy. Fear of failure? That's the real creativity killer.

When a project doesn't pan out, resist the urge to play the blame game. Instead, lean in with curiosity. Ask questions like, "What did we learn? What worked, and what didn't? How can we apply this next time?" When you do that, people start taking risks—and risks are where innovation lies. Missteps and failure are stepping stones, not sinkholes.

Imagine a workplace where people aren't frozen by the fear of getting it wrong. Where trying something new, even if it doesn't stick the landing, is encouraged. Where so-called "failure" is reframed as an opportunity to gather insights and refine ideas.

To be clear, I'm not saying you need to be overly

forgiving or avoid accountability. If the project failed because someone dropped the ball, they must be held responsible.

As a leader, your job isn't to prevent every potential error. It's to foster an environment where your team feels safe enough to take bold risks and explore uncharted territory.

The Long-Term Impact of Psychological Safety

When people do not have psychological safety, they play it safe. They keep their best ideas locked up tight. But when you create a space where people actually feel safe? Magic happens. Real, transformative magic. Magic that can set your university apart.

Imagine a team where people aren't just showing up, punching a clock, and counting down the minutes until five o'clock. Imagine a place where people are actually excited to solve problems. Where taking a risk doesn't feel risky. Psychological safety creates an environment where people know their voice matters and where mistakes are seen as learning, not failure.

The most innovative teams aren't perfect. They're brave. They're willing to try something that might not work. The risk is often worth the reward.

Your job as a leader isn't to control everything. It's to create space for something extraordinary to happen. To show your team that they're more than just cogs in a machine. And here's the wild part: when you do this when you actually see and hear your people, they'll move mountains for you. Not because they have to. Because they want to.

Prioritizing Well-Being

Employees aren't just workers—they're people. They have lives outside the office, with families, responsibilities, struggles, and dreams. When leaders forget that, it's obvious. Burnout creeps in. Morale takes a nosedive. Even the most dedicated team members start checking out.

Employees don't need cheesy perks or pizza parties. They need respect. Respect for their time, energy, and humanity. Start with workloads. If your team is drowning in unrealistic expectations—extended periods of 60-hour weeks, endless to-do lists—you're hurting productivity and sending a message that their well-being doesn't matter as much as their output. But when leaders set achievable goals and ensure teams are adequately staffed, it shows they care. When people feel cared for, they're more productive and more engaged. Supported employees want to give their best, not because they have to, but because they want to.

Flexibility is another game-changer. Life doesn't conveniently pause between 8 a.m. and 5 p.m. Kids get sick. Parents need help. Unexpected emergencies crop up. By offering flexible options like remote and hybrid schedules, adjustable hours, and the ability to step away when life demands it, you're giving employees something priceless: breathing room.

And then there's wellness. Real wellness isn't an occasional yoga session or a one-off email about stress management. It's a culture where self-care is baked into the day-to-day and encouraged. Early in my career, a peer took a mental health day, and our shared supervisor made it well known that they felt that it was unprofessional. In fact, they spent most of the day ensuring that all of the rest of us knew unscheduled mental health days were unacceptable.

In truth, it was the supervisor's behavior that wasn't acceptable. The message we all received loud and clear was this: your health and well-being don't matter. You are a cog in a machine that must always be running.

Transparency and Trust

When employees feel like decisions are made behind closed doors, it's more than just frustrating—it's unsettling. It leaves them guessing, wondering, "Why was that decision made? Who's pulling the strings? What aren't they telling us?" And once doubt creeps in, it's like a slow leak in a tire. It deflates trust, little by little, until nothing feels stable anymore. That's where transparency comes in.

Transparency is the signal leaders send when they communicate openly about what's happening, why, and how it affects the team. Whether clarifying reporting lines, explaining role expectations, or walking people through the reasoning behind a significant change, transparency says: *We respect you enough to keep you in the loop.* Respect is a big deal. People notice when they're treated as partners instead of bystanders.

If you're rolling out a change, take the time to explain the why. Why this decision? Why now? Why does it matter to the team? Connecting those dots helps people see the bigger picture and how they fit into it. When the reasoning behind decisions is clear, people feel less like they're being dragged along for the ride and more like they're part of the journey.

When you invite people to weigh in on decisions affecting their work, you do more than collect input. You're showing them their perspective matters. Knowing they were heard can make all the difference, even if the outcome isn't what someone hoped for. It shifts the narrative from, *"This is being done to me"* to "This is being done with me." That's a massive mindset shift that builds trust like nothing else.

Take structural changes, for instance. Maybe you're restructuring a team to improve efficiency. It will hit people like a gut punch if you announce it out of nowhere. But if you involve them early—by sharing the challenges you're trying to solve, asking for their insights, and keeping them in the loop—you turn what could feel like a top-down directive into a collaborative effort. People feel less blindsided and more invested. That's how you create buy-in. That's how you build trust.

And trust is the whole point. Transparency fosters a culture where everyone feels like they're on the same team. When employees feel informed and included, they're more engaged and more resilient. They're more willing to roll with the punches when things get tough because they trust the people leading the way.

Giving Feedback

Giving feedback isn't easy. It can feel like walking a tightrope. One wrong word, and you risk damaging morale. But feedback doesn't have to be a dreaded conversation. When done with empathy, it's an opportunity to help a team member grow and become their best self. How you approach these conversations says as much about your leadership as the words you choose.

Building on Strengths

The most effective feedback begins with what's right. Recognizing effort and highlighting successes isn't "being nice"; it reinforces the things that are already working. It shows that you see and value their contributions, which makes any constructive feedback feel like part of a bigger picture of growth.

You could frame feedback like this: "Your presentation was well-organized, and the visuals were spot-on. I think adding a bit more detail to your key points could make it even stronger." You're not tearing them down—you're helping them build up.

Reframing Feedback as a Collaboration

Instead of diving in with, "You missed the mark on this," try, "Let's look at this together and see how we can make it stronger." This approach focuses on the work rather than the individual, reducing defensiveness. You're not saying, "I'm here to judge you." You're saying, "I'm here to help you."

For example, if a team member submits a report with errors, resist the urge to point out the mistakes bluntly. Instead, invite a dialogue: "I noticed a few areas in the report that were inaccurate. Can we walk through what happened together?" That simple shift turns feedback into a shared effort.

Offering Support, Not Just Critique

Empathetic feedback doesn't stop at pointing out what needs to change. It's also asking, *How can I help?* When you offer support, you send a clear message: *I'm invested in your success.*

It might sound like, "I know this task has been challenging. What resources or support would help make it more manageable?" Maybe they need more clarity, better tools, or even encouragement that they are on the right track. By positioning yourself as a partner in their growth, you create an environment where feedback feels like guidance, not judgment.

And sometimes, it's as simple as showing you're in it with them. "Let's brainstorm some ideas together to tackle this issue" is one way to signal that feedback isn't just a directive—it's a collaboration.

Keeping the Conversation Going

Feedback isn't a one-and-done event. It's part of an ongoing relationship. Following up after you've given feedback shows that you care about more than just the problem. You care about their progress. It also reinforces positive change and helps solidify growth.

For example, if you've coached someone on improving their meeting facilitation, check in after their next attempt: "I noticed how you engaged everyone in the discussion today. It was a big improvement. How did you feel about it? Is there anything else I can help you refine?" These follow-ups make feedback a continuous loop of learning, growth, and recognition.

Spotting Fear

Sometimes, when someone on our team behaves in a way we didn't expect, our first instinct is to get upset or assign blame. But what often drives unexpected or counterproductive actions is fear. Fear is a powerful driver (think fear of judgment, fear of losing respect, fear of failing publicly). And if we recognize that fear, we can tackle what's really going on instead of just reacting to the outward behavior.

Don't just label them "difficult" or "unprofessional." Ask yourself what might be scaring them. Are they worried about looking stupid? About letting you down? Maybe they're terrified of not meeting the team's standards. When we tune into that anxiety, we see them in a more human way.

People need to feel safe enough to speak up. We create a safer environment when we acknowledge that fear might be behind their actions (instead of scolding them right away). Over time, they'll trust you more. And once trust is there, people speak more openly. They share ideas, concerns, and even failures—because they're not worried about punishment or shame.

When you figure out what someone's afraid of, you can help fix the root cause. That might mean clarifying their role, giving them more training, or setting smaller goals they can handle. The solutions become more personal and helpful—and everybody wins. Otherwise, we slap on bandaids that never really solve anything.

Looking for fear shows you respect people as complex individuals (with their worries and backstories). And that encourages more open conversations. Mistakes become lessons, not reasons to point fingers. It's a culture shift from fear-based to growth-based.

Tension Has Value

Tension and fear can feel similar in the heat of the moment, but they're not the same. Fear is that heavy feeling that stops us from moving forward (the kind that makes your stomach drop). Tension, on the other hand, can spark new ideas or push us to dig deeper. It's like the nervous energy before a big performance—it's unpleasant, but it can sharpen your focus and prepare you to act.

A little friction or disagreement can lead to breakthroughs. When everyone sees a problem from different angles, tension can push the best solution to the surface. Without any tension, things can get stale. Healthy tension nudges you out of your comfort zone. You learn, adapt, and improve because you have to.

But fear is different. Fear paralyzes. It makes people shut down or avoid taking risks. Tension, when managed well, is an asset. It's like a driving force that says, "Okay, we can do better, so let's figure it out." Fear says, "Don't even try."

So, embrace tension. Use it. Let it fuel your curiosity and push you to find better ways of doing things. But if you sense fear creeping in, that's a sign you need to pause, address what's causing it, and create the kind of environment where tension becomes motivation—not intimidation.

Supporting Your Team's Growth

Supporting growth means investing in people and seeing them not as static but as full of potential and capable of much more than their current job descriptions. People have ambitions. They have talents waiting to be uncovered and nurtured. As a leader, recognizing that is step one.

Growth starts with clarity. So many employees feel stuck, not because they don't have what it takes to grow but because they don't know how to get there. Imagine trying to climb a ladder you can't even see. By clearly defining roles and pathways forward, leaders give employees something solid to stand on—a foundation for growth. But it doesn't end there. People need more than the "what." They need the "how." They need to know what skills to build, what opportunities to chase, and how success is measured. A career roadmap is a way of saying, "We see your potential, and we're here to help you get there."

Mentorship is another game-changer. Think back to someone who guided you early in your career. Pretty impactful, right? Leaders who prioritize mentorship create those same opportunities for their teams. Pairing junior employees with seasoned mentors or offering formal coaching programs gives people someone in their corner, rooting for their success. When people know someone has their back, their confidence and engagement skyrocket.

But growth isn't always a straight path. It's messy. Sometimes, people want to stretch their wings, explore new interests, or pivot to a different role. Empathetic leaders get that. They build flexibility into their structures—temporary assignments, cross-department projects, or stretch roles—to give employees room to experiment.

People thrive on acknowledgment. When someone masters a new skill, leads a big project, or earns a promotion, it's worth recognizing. It doesn't have to be flashy—a quick shoutout in a meeting, a heartfelt email, or a handwritten note can go a long way. These moments say, "We see you. We appreciate you. You're growing, and we're proud of you." Simple? Yes. Powerful? Absolutely.

Not everyone starts at the same place, and barriers to growth are real. Empathetic leaders don't just shrug and hope for the best. They actively seek out and address the challenges holding some people back—bias, lack of access to resources, uneven workloads, you name it. They ensure opportunities are distributed fairly so everyone, regardless of background or role, has a chance to advance. Because growth that isn't equitable isn't really growth at all.

When employees see that their growth genuinely matters, they show up with more purpose and enthusiasm. They see their work as part of something bigger than just a paycheck.

Balancing Autonomy and Support

People thrive when they feel trusted to do their jobs. That's the magic of autonomy—it allows people to experiment with new ideas and solve problems on their own terms. But autonomy isn't the same as being left to fend for yourself. It's not, "Here's your project, good luck figuring it out." You need to strike a perfect balance between giving freedom and offering support.

Autonomy without support is like handing someone a map but forgetting the compass. They might get to the destination eventually, but it will be a much more arduous journey—and they'll probably feel lost (and maybe even a little abandoned) along the way. On the flip side, too much support can quickly veer into micromanagement. Nothing stifles creativity or motivation faster than feeling like every move you make is being scrutinized.

Empathetic leadership finds the sweet spot. It starts with trust—showing your team your belief in their ability to handle the job. Trust says, *"I hired you because you're good at what you do, and I don't need to second-guess every decision you make."* But trust isn't enough on its own. Don't toss people into the deep end with a "sink or swim" mentality. Pair that trust with the tools and guidance they need to succeed.

So, how do you set someone up for success without hovering? It could mean establishing clear expectations upfront—what the goals are, what success looks like—and then stepping back to let them figure out the best way to get there. Or giving someone the freedom to tackle a major project but scheduling regular check-ins. Not to micromanage but to offer feedback and provide the occasional course correction if needed.

Autonomy only works when the structure around it makes sense. If the environment is chaotic or the goals are unclear, autonomy can quickly feel like being set adrift. No one thrives when they're constantly wondering, *"Am I doing this right? Is this what they expect?"* Clarity is essential. Ensure your team understands how their work fits into the bigger picture. With that foundation in place, autonomy doesn't feel like being left alone—it feels like being empowered.

When you get this balance right, people start taking ownership. They get bolder with their ideas. They push boundaries, knowing they have the support to navigate challenges and the freedom to innovate.

Creativity takes courage. And courage takes support. In my pre-CMO days, I was lucky enough to work for a leader who gave me near-total autonomy — but had my back when I needed it. Over the five years I spent there, my scrappy team and I accomplished fantastic work, like launching one of higher education's first fully mobile websites, a cutting-edge app that had features way ahead of its time, and an interactive campus tour well before most of higher ed had caught on. That innovation was only possible because we had freedom *and* support.

Stop Micromanaging

Micromanagement is a trap that even the best-intentioned leaders can fall into. It usually starts from a good place—

wanting to ensure quality, hit deadlines, or avoid mistakes. But the fallout from micromanaging can be brutal. It drains creativity, erodes trust, and leaves employees feeling like their contributions don't matter. Nobody thrives when they feel like someone is constantly looking over their shoulder.

The irony? The more you micromanage, the more likely you are to create the very problems you're trying to prevent. Teams get stuck in a cycle of hesitation, second-guessing every move because they fear doing it "wrong." And instead of encouraging progress, you end up bottle-necking decisions and burning yourself out in the process. It's a lose-lose for everyone.

Micromanagement might seem like control, but it's actually the opposite. It creates chaos. To lead effectively, you've got to step back, trust your people, and shift your focus to fostering independence and collaboration. Find the balance that lets your team shine while you still steer the ship in the right direction.

It can be challenging to recognize micromanagement tendencies in yourself. Here are some red flags to watch for:

- You frequently check in on minor details or demand constant updates.
- You struggle to let team members make decisions without your input.
- You find yourself redoing or "fixing" work already completed.
- Your team seems hesitant to take initiative or share ideas.
- You feel exhausted and overwhelmed because you're trying to control too much.

Leaders micromanage for all kinds of reasons, and most of them make sense at the moment. Maybe they're worried about how mistakes will reflect on them. After all, when you're in charge, it can feel like every misstep has your name written all over it. Or maybe they're terrified of failure—convinced that something critical will slip through the cracks if they don't oversee every detail. And then there's the classic: "No one else can do it as well as I can." (Spoiler alert: they probably can, and sometimes even better.)

These worries are natural, but micromanaging doesn't fix them. They stifle initiative instead of empowering their team to operate independently and confidently. People stop taking ownership of their work because why bother? If every decision gets second-guessed, it's easier to just wait for instructions than risk stepping on the wrong toes. And that's when you start to see creativity, innovation, and even basic motivation take a nosedive.

So, while it's understandable to want to keep a tight grip on things, it's worth asking yourself: Is this about protecting the project or my own sense of control?

Breaking free from micromanaging isn't easy. It takes self-awareness, a healthy dose of trust, and a real commitment to empowering your team. But the payoff is worth it. When you let go of that need to control every detail, you create space for your team to shine and free yourself up to focus on the bigger picture. Here's how to get started:

- **Shift Your Focus to the Big Picture:** Your job as a leader isn't to comb through every email draft or obsess over the color of a chart. It's to set the vision, provide the tools, and clear the

path so your team can succeed. When you catch yourself diving into the weeds, take a step back. Ask yourself, "Am I focusing on the strategic goals or getting lost in the execution?" Execution isn't your job anymore. Trust your team to handle it. They're probably more than capable.
- **Learn to Delegate the Right Way:** Delegation doesn't mean dumping tasks on people so you can cross them off your list. It means giving your team meaningful responsibilities and trusting them to handle them. Start by being super clear about what you're looking for. What's the outcome you want? What tools or resources do they need to get there? Then, and this is the hard part, let them run with it. Stay available for questions, but resist the urge to hover. Delegation done right isn't just a productivity hack—it's how you show your team that you believe in them.
- **Build Trust with Open Communication:** Micromanaging often comes from fear. Fear that things will go wrong, that mistakes will reflect poorly on you, or that your team doesn't know what they're doing. The antidote to that fear? Communication. Talk to your team. Set clear expectations upfront, and don't wait until something goes wrong to offer feedback. Let them know it's okay to ask questions or flag concerns. When you're open and approachable, you'll find that trust flows both ways. (And yes, trust is earned, but someone has to go first. Why not you?)

- **Stop Fixing What Doesn't Need Fixing:** Not everything needs to be done *your way*. Let me say that again for the perfectionists in the back: if the work gets the job done, it doesn't have to look exactly like you'd imagined. Sure, you might tweak a font or reword a sentence, but ask yourself, "Does this change actually matter?" Nine times out of ten, the answer is no. Let it go. Save your energy for the stuff that really moves the needle.
- **Empower Your Team to Step Up**: When people feel trusted and supported, they're more likely to take ownership of their work—and crush it. Create an environment where your team feels confident and capable. Offer training or development opportunities so they can level up their skills. Celebrate big and small wins and let them know their efforts are noticed. And when they stumble (because everyone does), approach it as a learning moment, not a failure.

Breaking the micromanagement habit requires you to shift from doing everything yourself to creating a team that can thrive without constant oversight. When you lead with trust and empower your people, you'll be amazed at what they can accomplish and how much more time and mental energy you'll have to focus on what matters.

Neglectful Management: The Silent Killer

Neglectful management might not grab headlines like its flashier counterpart, micromanagement, but it's just as damaging (and maybe even more so). Micromanagement stems from over-involvement, while neglectful management comes from absence—failing to provide the support, resources, or direction your team needs to thrive. It's easy to fall into this trap, especially when juggling a thousand priorities. But neglect can quietly wreak havoc on your team, leaving employees feeling unsupported.

Picture this scenario: an employee shows up, eager to do their job and make a difference. They are left without clear expectations, goals, or the tools they need to do their job effectively. They ask questions but get vague answers—or worse, none at all. They work hard, but no one notices or acknowledges their contributions. And when they hit a roadblock, there's no one there to help navigate it. Over time, that eagerness turns into frustration, then apathy. It's not long before they're mentally checked out—or checking out job postings.

Neglect doesn't just demotivate employees; it actively disengages them. Without support or direction, productivity tanks, performance suffers, and morale plummets. Employees start questioning their value to the organization —or if they have any. And here's the kicker: neglect erodes trust and respect between managers and their teams, poisoning the culture and setting the stage for high turnover.

Breaking the Cycle of Neglect

Once you've developed neglectful habits (we all slip up sometimes), correcting it can be challenging. But it's not impossible. Small, intentional changes can make a world of difference. Here's how to start:

- **Be Present and Available:** Make it clear to your team that you're there for them. This doesn't mean having an open-door policy 24/7 (boundaries matter), but it does mean being responsive and approachable when they need support.
- **Set Clear Expectations:** Ambiguity breeds frustration. Take the time to outline goals, priorities, and responsibilities. When people know what's expected of them, they can focus their energy where it matters most.
- **Provide Resources and Training:** Ensure your team has what they need to succeed. This could be anything from new software to professional development opportunities. Investing in their growth shows you're invested in them.
- **Acknowledge Contributions:** Recognition doesn't have to be grand or expensive. A simple "Great job on that project" or "I really appreciate the effort you put into this" can go a long way in making someone feel valued.
- **Tackle Problems Head-On:** Ignoring issues won't make them disappear (spoiler alert: it makes them worse). If an employee raises a concern, address it promptly and transparently. Proactive problem-solving builds trust and shows you care.
- **Listen, Really Listen:** Encourage open communication and take the time to hear what your team has to say. Whether it's feedback, ideas, or frustrations, listening validates their experiences and creates a stronger connection.

Neglect isn't just a management issue—it's a people issue. A neglected employee feels invisible, and no one thrives in that kind of environment. The cost? Stress, burnout, and eventually, attrition. Talented team members will leave for places where they feel supported and appreciated (and who can blame them?).

If you're worried you might be veering into neglectful territory, start with a little self-reflection. Ask yourself: Am I giving my team the time, attention, and resources they need to do their best work? If the answer is "not really" or "sometimes," that's okay. Awareness is the first step toward change.

Insights and Impact Plan

Hype-Free Insights

- **Psychological Safety Spurs Innovation:** Environments where people feel safe sharing ideas, taking risks, and admitting mistakes, foster creativity and collaboration.
- **Leadership Shapes the Culture:** Leaders create psychological safety by modeling vulnerability, admitting mistakes, and fostering open dialogue.
- **Empathy Enhances Engagement:** Listening, validating emotions, and demonstrating genuine care for team members' experiences encourage openness, loyalty, and a more connected workplace.

- **Clear Expectations and Consistency Build Trust:** Transparent, fair, and consistent guidelines ensure accountability and prevent ambiguity, promoting stability and mutual respect within teams.
- **Constructive Feedback Fuels Growth:** Empathetic feedback that emphasizes strengths, involves collaboration and provides support, fosters development, and builds confidence.
- **Recognition Reinforces a Growth Mindset:** Celebrating contributions and lessons learned from failures encourages innovation, reduces fear, and promotes a team culture that thrives on experimentation.

Impact Plan

- **Create Opportunities for Idea-Sharing**: Implement forums, such as weekly brainstorming sessions or dedicated Slack channels, where team members can share and refine ideas without judgment.
- **Model Vulnerability as a Leader:** Share personal challenges, mistakes, and learning experiences with your team to foster trust and encourage open communication.
- **Reframe Feedback Conversations:** Approach feedback collaboratively by focusing on strengths and partnering with team members to find solutions, emphasizing their growth potential.
- **Recognize and Celebrate Contributions:** Develop a system for acknowledging successes

and the lessons learned from failures, whether through team meetings, shout-outs, or personal notes.
- **Set Clear Goals and Communicate Transparently:** Regularly review and communicate expectations, progress, and any changes to ensure alignment and accountability.
- **Invest in Team Well-being**: Encourage flexibility, provide adequate resources, and support mental health initiatives to demonstrate a commitment to employees' well-being.
- **Evaluate and Address Fear-Based Dynamics:** Identify and address root causes of fear in the workplace, replacing them with practices that encourage tension as a productive driver for innovation rather than a deterrent.

Chapter 11
Finding the Leader You're Meant to Be

Early in my career, I returned from a conference bursting with excitement. My notebook was packed with ideas—some bold and ambitious, others simple tweaks I thought could have a big impact. Most were budget-neutral and wouldn't be heavy lifts, but I believed they could dramatically improve our approach to public relations and storytelling. During a one-on-one meeting with my supervisor, I eagerly shared my thoughts, expecting encouragement or, at the very least, curiosity. Instead, my usually very supportive boss sat across from me, stone-faced.

When I paused, hoping for feedback, he delivered a response I'll never forget: "I don't pay you for ideas. I pay you to do what I tell you to do."

The words hit me like a gut punch. My stomach churned, and I felt the sharp sting of tears threatening to spill. Until then, I had built my career on being an idea generator who thrived on innovation and problem-solving. A previous supervisor once told me, "Managing you is easy. I get out of the way and watch you create new worlds." Hearing that my ideas weren't wanted felt like a rejection of who I was as a professional. I felt chastised for even considering having an independent thought.

Something shifted in me after that conversation. I began showing up differently—quieter, less eager, more guarded. As someone motivated by creation and innovation, I felt like I was locking up a central part of my being. Six months later, I left that job. In hindsight, I believe my boss was having a bad day, but that moment taught me an unforgettable lesson: one careless interaction can cost you a high-performing team member.

That moment with my supervisor taught me more about leadership than any seminar or book ever could. It showed me how fragile morale can be and how crucial it is for leaders to approach their roles with empathy. One careless comment can dampen creativity, but a moment of encouragement can ignite it. Leaders have the power to shape the work that gets done and how people feel while doing it. And when you lead with empathy, the results speak for themselves: stronger teams, better ideas, and workplaces people don't want to leave.

Growing Into an Empathetic Leader

Before you can lead anyone else, you've got to start with yourself. What sets you off? What patterns keep showing up in how you communicate? What values drive the way you make decisions? Leading others effectively will always feel tenuous if you can't answer these questions.

Leadership requires both a big-picture vision and attention to the small, everyday moments—how you respond to challenges and the way you show up when no one's watching. Those moments are shaped by who you are at your core.

Self-reflection is an important way to reconnect with your values and strengths. What do you stand for? What kind of leader do you want to be? Maybe you value collaboration over competition. Or maybe integrity and accountability are your north stars. Whatever it is, knowing your core values keeps you grounded. It's like having a compass —when things get messy (and they always do), you have something solid to guide you.

Sometimes, asking questions is the best way to understand yourself as a leader. Spend some time reflecting on these prompts:

- **"When was the last time I felt truly 'in my element' at work?"** Think about a moment when you felt energized and effective. What were you doing? Who was involved? What skills were you using? This can reveal what fuels your passion and aligns with your natural leadership strengths.
- **"How do I respond when someone challenges my ideas?"** Be honest. Do you lean into collaboration, or do you get defensive? Do you listen fully or start preparing your counterargument mid-sentence? Reflecting on this can help you understand how open you are to feedback and where there's room for growth.
- **"What's one leadership habit I'm proud of—and one I'm not?"** Celebrate the strengths you bring to the table and identify areas where you could show up differently. What's something you wish you handled better last week or last year?

- **"How do I want people to feel after interacting with me?"** The old adage that says people don't remember what you say; they remember how you made them feel is so true. Are you intentional about how your actions and words shape the environment around you?
- **"What makes me snap at someone when I'm normally calm?"** Is it the pressure of a looming deadline? A meeting that runs long? Or maybe it's something subtler, like feeling unheard or unappreciated.

Crafting Your Mission Statement

A leadership mission statement defines your vision in a few sentences. It should capture who you are and how you want to lead.

To get started:

- **Reflect on your values.** What do you stand for as a leader? Is it collaboration, integrity, creativity, or something else?
- **Think about your goals.** What kind of impact do you want to have on your team, organization, or community?
- **Combine the two** into a concise, inspiring statement.

Example:

"I lead with curiosity and integrity, fostering environments where people feel valued, heard, and empowered to grow. I aim to create meaningful connections and help others achieve their full potential."

Your mission statement should feel personal and true to you. It's your compass, something to revisit when challenges arise or you need to refocus.

Self-reflection takes time and a little discomfort. It's not always fun to realize you've been short with someone because you were in a bad mood or your "open door" policy isn't as open as you thought. But in those moments of honesty with yourself, you start noticing patterns. That gives you a chance to become the kind of leader people trust and respect.

The Skills of a Great Leader

Empathetic leadership is a lifelong process. The best leaders know that there's always room for improvement, and they actively seek it. They learn from their successes *and* their missteps. Positive leadership is a commitment to the journey. Here are some important skills to hone:

Self-Awareness

Leadership always starts with you. Your words, actions, and energy set the tone for your team. Self-awareness means paying attention to how you show up, how your moods influence the room, how your decisions impact others, and how your leadership style either lifts people up or holds them back. When people are self-aware, they are more mindful. They reflect on their strengths and weaknesses, allowing them to lead with authenticity and intention. Take time to reflect. Ask for feedback. Be willing to grow.

Resilience

Challenges are inevitable. Things will go sideways, and the unexpected will throw you off course. Resilience is what keeps you grounded. Resilience gives you the ability to stay steady in the storm, not by pretending everything is fine but by showing your team that obstacles are opportunities to learn and adapt. When you are resilient, you can do more than bounce back. You find ways to bounce forward and grow stronger with every challenge. When your team sees you staying optimistic and solution-focused, they'll follow your lead.

Confidence

People instinctively look for confidence in a leader. When you project confidence, you inspire it in others. Your team feels more secure knowing you've got a steady hand on the wheel, even when the path ahead isn't clear. Confidence also means making decisions with conviction (and owning them, even if they don't pan out perfectly). It's the quiet assurance that says, "We'll get through this together."

A Positive Mindset

I'm not talking about toxic positivity or naive optimism. I'm talking about the belief that there's always a way forward, even when things feel impossible. Gratitude plays a big role here. Taking time to appreciate the good—your team's efforts, small wins, the lessons learned from setbacks—shifts the focus from what's wrong to what's possible. Positivity is contagious. When you look for the silver linings and lead with hope, you give your team permission to do the same.

Finding Your Leadership Style

Developing an empathetic leadership style requires deliberate choices and self-reflection. Ask yourself: How do I respond to new ideas, even when stressed? Do I actively listen, or am I quick to dismiss? Am I creating a culture where team members feel safe to bring their whole selves to work?

Empathetic leadership is showing up with intention, fostering positivity even in difficult moments, and recognizing that every word and action shapes your team's culture. A single interaction—good or bad—can leave a lasting impact.

No two empathetic leaders look exactly alike. Your style should reflect your strengths, but at its core, your style should always be rooted in bringing out the best in others. Here are a few styles to consider:

The Inspirer

You're the leader who sees the forest through the trees—and helps everyone else see it, too. Your strength lies in painting a compelling vision of the future, something that gets your team excited about what they're working toward. You don't just talk about goals; you bring them to life, showing how the work today connects to the possibilities of tomorrow. When a project feels overwhelming, or the path forward isn't clear, you remind your team of the "why."

An Inspirer makes vision tangible. You set the direction, but you also light the way, giving your team the motivation and clarity they need to push forward. Whether it's rallying the group at the start of a new initiative or reinvigorating morale when challenges arise, your ability to inspire helps your team stay focused and energized.

The Harmonizer

Conflict doesn't scare you. You see it as an opportunity to build bridges. As a Harmonizer, you have a knack for bringing people together, even when things get messy. You're the one who steps in when tensions rise, not to take sides but to foster understanding. By listening and seeing all perspectives, you help your team move beyond disagreements and focus on what really matters.

You don't just smooth over conflicts; you create an environment where people feel safe to speak their minds and trust that their voices will be heard—respectfully. Your leadership style creates an environment where everyone's unique strengths combine into something even greater.

The Coach

You're the type of leader who sees potential everywhere you look. You're deeply invested in your team's growth and take the time to understand each person's goals and aspirations. When you give feedback, it's focused on helping your team members grow into the best versions of themselves.

Whether you're guiding someone through a tough challenge or celebrating their achievements, your focus is always on development. You know that when individuals thrive, the whole team benefits. Your approach builds loyalty and trust, creating a culture where people feel supported and empowered to take risks and stretch their abilities.

The Collaborator

You're the glue that holds it all together. While others might get stuck in their silos, you see the value in connection. You actively seek out diverse perspectives, recognizing that the best solutions come from bringing more voices to the table. As a Collaborator, you thrive on teamwork, encouraging open dialogue and creative problem-solving.

You're the leader who says, "Let's figure this out together," and then rolls up your sleeves to make it happen. You create systems and spaces where collaboration isn't just possible—it's easy. Your ability to unite people with varying expertise and viewpoints builds a sense of belonging and shared purpose that strengthens the team.

The Anchor

You're the steady hand in the storm. When everything feels chaotic, you remain calm and grounded. As an Anchor, you provide stability and reassurance to your team, helping them confidently navigate uncertainty. Your presence is a reminder that no matter what happens, you'll figure it out together.

This leadership style is invaluable in times of crisis or high-pressure situations. While others might react impulsively, you take a thoughtful, measured approach, ensuring decisions are made with care. Your reliability builds trust and loyalty, creating a team that feels secure even when the stakes are high.

The Listener

You create space for others to share their thoughts and ideas. As a Listener, your superpower is your ability to really hear what people are saying—not only the words but the emotions and intentions behind them. You ensure that everyone feels seen and heard and often bring clarity to situations by synthesizing different viewpoints.

Your calm, reflective nature creates a safe environment where people share openly. While other leaders might focus on leading the charge, you focus on developing understanding, often leading to deeper, more thoughtful solutions.

You don't have to pick just one style. Blend them to fit your team's needs and your organization's goals. Lead authentically, and your style will shine.

The Power of Positive Communication

How you communicate shapes culture. Every interaction and every gesture sends a message about what you value and how you lead. A single conversation can leave someone feeling empowered and inspired or cast a shadow that lingers long after the meeting ends. That's why positive communication is so powerful. Let's break it down.

Set the Example

Positivity starts with you. Your tone, body language, and how you react under pressure influence your team's dynamic. If you approach challenges with optimism and resilience, your team is more likely to do the same. Model the energy you want to see. Smile when you greet someone (it makes a difference). Keep your body language open.

Speak in a calm, measured tone, even when the conversation gets tough. Positivity is contagious, and it starts at the top.

Celebrate Wins

Don't underestimate the power of recognition. Did someone go above and beyond on a project? Call it out. Did a team overcome a tough challenge? Acknowledge it publicly. It doesn't have to be elaborate. A genuine "I see what you did, and it matters" can mean the world. Recognition fuels motivation and reminds your team that their hard work is noticed.

Be Transparent

Positivity doesn't mean sugarcoating feedback. Being honest about expectations builds trust. When your team knows you'll level with them, they feel secure—even when the news isn't great. Transparency doesn't just create clarity; it shows respect. Share the "why" behind decisions. Explain the bigger picture. Invite questions, and don't be afraid to admit when you don't have all the answers. When people feel included in the conversation, they're more likely to stay engaged and invested.

The Magic of Feeling Seen.

People want to feel valued. They want to know that their contributions matter and their voices are heard. Positive communication creates that connection. It's in the way you listen when someone speaks. It's how you ask for input or check in to see how someone's doing. When people feel seen and appreciated, they bring their best selves to work.

The Joy of Guiding the Next Generation of Leaders

When I started at WSSU, the executive assistant to one of the deans asked if we could meet so she could learn more about my background and career trajectory. During our conversation, Lea (not her real name) shared that she held undergraduate and graduate degrees in communications and public relations and was eager to shift her career in that direction. I was impressed by her passion and professionalism and mentally tagged her as someone I'd love to have on my team one day.

When a communications specialist position opened up, I encouraged Lea to apply. It quickly became apparent that she was the best candidate, and we welcomed her to the team. To my delight, Lea brought more than just the right skill set—she was a savvy diplomat who could deftly navigate conflicts within the department. Her experience as an executive assistant gave her a knack for finding creative, efficient solutions to problems.

To support her growth, I assigned her increasingly complex projects. In every instance, she excelled. Within a year, Lea reported directly to me and became one of my most trusted advisors. When I left WSSU for Miami University, she had transformed into a confident, creative professional.

But our story didn't end there. A few months after I started at Miami, an executive communications position opened up on my team. I immediately thought of Lea. She was a masterful writer, and her personality and skills made her well-suited to working directly with senior leadership. When the president met her, he agreed—and Lea relocated to Ohio to join the team.

Within months, the president recognized Lea's thoughtfulness and expertise, asking me if I would mind if he added her to the Cabinet. I couldn't have been more thrilled! This was a chance for more people to see what an amazing professional Lea was.

Although I left Miami about 18 months later, I've continued to watch Lea's career with immense pride. She has been promoted twice since I departed and is now thriving as a senior leader at the university.

One of the most rewarding parts of being in senior leadership is watching someone with raw potential like Lea evolve into a confident, capable professional. And it's incredibly gratifying when you get to help them get there. Investing your time and energy into mentoring someone who might one day take your place might seem counterintuitive. But there's nothing quite like seeing an early-career professional step into their own, ready to tackle challenges they didn't dream they could tackle.

If you've been in leadership long enough, you know how to spot team members with that extra spark—the drive, the curiosity, the hunger to grow. These individuals don't just want to do their jobs; they want to excel. Recognizing talent is one thing—nurturing it takes effort. It requires intention and a willingness to invest in their future. But the payoff isn't just theirs—it's yours, too. Watching them succeed becomes one of the great joys of your career.

Give Them Room to Stretch

Your role as a senior leader is vast—budget oversight, personnel management, and setting a vision for your team. But for someone earlier in their career, the scope of your work can seem a little mysterious (and maybe even intimidating). That's where you step in.

Find opportunities for them to step outside their comfort zone. Assign projects that stretch their skills, especially in areas they don't typically tackle. For example, if they're great at execution but haven't led strategy, involve them in planning sessions. If they've never managed a budget, let them sit in on your process and ask questions. And if you think they're ready, give them control over smaller projects or initiatives. The goal isn't to throw them into the deep end but to let them dip their toes into new waters.

Let Them Handle the Tough Stuff

Sometimes, you need to take a step back. When conflicts arise, or challenges bubble up within the team, it's tempting to swoop in and fix everything. After all, that's part of what leaders do, right? But stepping aside can be just as important.

When you let a rising leader handle tough management challenges, you allow them to develop maturity, poise, and problem-solving skills. Of course, you're not leaving them to figure it all out alone. Sit down with them beforehand. Walk through the situation, discuss potential approaches, and let them decide how to proceed. Will they handle everything perfectly? Probably not. But every mistake and misstep will be a chance to grow. And isn't that the point?

Be Honest, Even When It's Hard

Mentorship doesn't work without trust. And trust comes from honesty. Yes, it's important to be positive and encouraging. But sugarcoating feedback does no one any favors. When you see room for improvement, say so—kindly, constructively, but candidly.

This is where your relationship with them matters most. If you've built a foundation of mutual respect, they'll know your critiques come from a place of wanting them to succeed. Failure can be one of the best teachers. Let them experiment. Let them take calculated risks. Even if they fall short, they'll learn something valuable they can carry forward.

"But What If They Leave?"

You might think, "If I pour my energy into developing this person, won't they just leave for a bigger opportunity?" Maybe. But holding someone back just to keep them around isn't a win for anyone. Not for you, not for them, and certainly not for your organization.

Instead, think about what you gain by being a leader who helps others grow. You build loyalty and commitment. You create a reputation as someone who invests in people. And even if they do move on, they'll remember you as a pivotal part of their journey.

Insights and Impact Plan

Hype-Free Insights

- **Empathy is a Leadership Superpower:** Empathetic leadership fosters trust, creativity, and engagement by demonstrating genuine care and adopting a collaborative mindset.
- **Positive Communication Shapes Culture:** Every interaction conveys values and influences morale. Leaders who communicate with positivity and transparency inspire loyalty and motivation.
- **Self-Awareness is Foundational:** Understanding how your moods, decisions, and actions affect your team allows for intentional and authentic leadership.
- **Resilience and Positivity Inspire Teams:** Resilience helps navigate challenges with composure, while a positive mindset focuses on possibilities, fostering hope and action among team members.
- **Growth-Oriented Leadership is Rewarding:** Mentoring and guiding the next generation of leaders benefits the individuals, the team, and the organization, creating a legacy of success.
- **Confidence Builds Trust and Enables Progress:** Confidence involves decisiveness, owning mistakes, and instilling assurance in your team's capabilities, fostering trust and security.

Impact Plan

- **Cultivate Empathy in Daily Interactions:** Practice active listening, validate emotions, and

adopt a "we'll figure this out together" mindset to build trust and engagement.
- **Identify and Lean into Your Leadership Style:** Reflect on your strengths and determine how to blend styles to best serve your team's needs and goals.
- **Encourage Growth Among Team Members:** Provide stretch assignments, offer honest feedback, and allow team members to handle challenging situations with your guidance.
- **Practice Self-Awareness and Reflection:** Regularly assess how your leadership impacts your team, seek feedback, and make adjustments to lead with greater intention and authenticity.

Chapter 12
The Architecture of Innovation

When most people hear "organizational structure," they picture a chart with names and job titles neatly stacked in rows and boxes. But structure is so much more than lines and labels. It's the framework that shapes how people work together—or don't. It's the invisible thread that either pulls people into connection or tangles them up in isolation.

Culture and structure are inseparable. What an organization values—whether that's innovation, collaboration, or clinging to the way it's always been—is reflected in its design. Take traditional hierarchies as an example. Yes, they clarify who answers to whom, but they often come at a cost. Departments turn inward, focused on their own goals and protecting their turf. Communication slows to a crawl, and collaboration becomes an afterthought. It's a setup that breeds silos, where everyone is rowing their own boat, but no one's sure which direction the fleet is supposed to go. The result is a culture that feels fractured and anything but inspiring.

But a culture built with empathy as its foundation moves

away from hierarchy for hierarchy's sake. It creates pathways for collaboration. A structure like this tells the team, "We trust your expertise, and we're designing this organization to help you succeed." When people feel supported, they don't just show up to do the bare minimum. They care. They innovate. They build momentum. And when that happens, the entire institution rises.

Structure also changes how an organization handles the unexpected. Challenges can hit from every direction—think enrollment drops, public relations nightmares, or global crises. A rigid structure can be a liability, slowing everything down and leaving people waiting for decisions to trickle down from the top. But when teams are trusted to pivot quickly and empowered to make decisions, the institution becomes more agile. It moves with the times instead of getting bogged down by them. And in the process, employees feel seen and valued. They know they're trusted to step up, which creates a culture where people thrive.

Practical Ways to Think About Org Structure

Before making changes or assessing the effectiveness of an organizational structure, consider how it impacts the people within it. Ask yourself:

- Are reporting lines clear, or do they create confusion or unnecessary tension?
- Are workloads evenly distributed, or are certain roles or teams consistently overburdened?
- Are there bottlenecks or communication gaps that frustrate employees or slow progress?
- Are people in roles that align with their skills, strengths, and career goals?

- Are there opportunities for individuals to grow or take on new challenges within the structure?
- Are there structural barriers that make communication between teams or departments difficult?
- Does the structure unintentionally favor certain groups or roles over others?
- Does the structure allow for timely decision-making, especially in fast-moving situations?
- Does the structure help employees see how their work contributes to the institution's mission?

Designing for Connection

Silos kill collaboration. When departments or teams operate in isolation, opportunities to share knowledge and ideas are lost. An empathetic structure creates pathways for connection. Consider:

- Forming cross-functional teams to tackle specific challenges.
- Creating regular opportunities for departments to share their work with one another.

The goal is to break down barriers, enabling team members to see themselves as part of a larger mission rather than isolated cogs in a machine.

For example, consider aligning the public relations and enrollment marketing teams on communications strategies. A story that the news team might write about a research project in the biology department could become part of a recruitment email for prospective students interested in biology. Or a piece highlighting the career services office could be repurposed for a campaign targeting parents anxious about their child finding a job after graduation.

This kind of synergy shouldn't be left to chance. It needs to be fostered by a structure that prioritizes collaboration and shared goals across departments.

Removing Barriers to Inclusion

Not all employees experience the workplace equally, and that's where empathy becomes a transformative leadership practice. Leaders need to actively examine how organizational structures impact access and equity. You can't just sit back and assume that everything works for everyone. You dig deeper. You ask questions. You listen to the people who might not feel included or supported. And then you do the hard work to change what's not working.

Who is in the room when big decisions are being made? (And who's noticeably not?) Too often, big decisions happen in a bubble—a small, homogenous group of people calling the shots while other perspectives and lived experiences are left out. That's a problem. When you're not expanding the table, you're missing opportunities. Empathetic leaders get this. They make it a priority to invite input from people across levels, departments, and backgrounds. Not as a token gesture but because they know it leads to better decisions. When people feel their voices matter, they're more likely to trust leadership and stay engaged.

Empathy also means critically assessing how work is distributed. Are opportunities for advancement spread fairly? Are some people getting overlooked for leadership roles or mentorship because they don't "fit the mold"? Informal systems, like mentorship networks, often favor certain groups while leaving others out. And invisible labor—like emotional support or tedious admin work—tends to fall disproportionately on women and people of color. Leaders need to step in to fix this. Formalize mentorship programs, ensure balanced workloads, and reimagine hiring and promotion practices to level the playing field.

Then there's policy. Policies can seem fair at first glance but still create barriers in practice. For example, a blanket remote work policy might work great for some employees while leaving others—like those who rely on in-person collaboration or support—at a disadvantage. The same goes for rigid schedules that don't account for working parents or caregivers. Leaders must ask, "Who might this policy exclude? How can we make it more inclusive?"

Change Management and Communication Strategies

Change is rarely a smooth process, especially the kind that shakes up structures and workflows. It can leave even the most capable team members feeling off balance. People thrive on routine and predictability; it gives them a sense of control. When change comes barreling through, it can fundamentally shift how team members see their roles and value within the organization. That's a lot to process.

Structural changes, in particular, are like rearranging the foundation of a building while people are still inside it. Suddenly, the familiar workflows and hierarchies they've relied on no longer work the same way. Teams might feel disconnected, unsure of who to report to or how their contributions fit into the bigger picture. Power dynamics can shift. Unspoken rules and norms might get thrown into question. And amid all this, people's confidence in the organization—and even in themselves—can take a hit.

Change doesn't have to equal chaos. Disruption can be a gateway to growth and opportunity with the right approach. It all comes down to thoughtful management and clear communication. Thoughtful management means slowing down enough to consider the logistics of the change *and* the human impact. Who's most affected? Where might they feel confused, anxious, or overwhelmed? And what support do they need to navigate this shift successfully?

Clear communication is the other half of the equation. People can handle a lot if they trust they are kept in the loop. They want to know what's happening, why, and how it will affect them. Silence breeds speculation, cynicism, and resistance. By communicating early and often and sharing the "why," you can help people find their footing even as the ground shifts beneath them.

Leadership Engagement: Model the Change You Want to See

Change starts at the top. If leaders don't embody the behaviors and mindsets needed for the new structure, why should anyone else? Leaders need to show through their actions that they're committed to the new way of working. This means being open to feedback, collaborating across silos, and being transparent during uncertain times. When leaders embrace change visibly and authentically, it sets the tone for everyone else to follow.

Transparency: Communicate Early, Often, and Honestly

People don't resist change because they hate new ideas; they resist it because they fear the unknown. The more you can reduce uncertainty, the smoother the process will be. Start by communicating what's changing and, more importantly, *why* it's changing. Lay out the problems you're solving, the goals you're aiming for, and how the new structure supports those goals.

Be honest about what you don't know yet. People can handle ambiguity if they trust you're being upfront. And don't treat communication as a one-and-done. Regular updates help keep everyone in the loop and reinforce the message that this is a shared journey, not a top-down decree.

Involving Employees Early: Bring People to the Table

Too often, decisions are made in a bubble, with leadership teams planning changes without input from the people who will live with them. This is a recipe for resentment and missed insights. Inviting employees into the planning process shows you value their expertise and perspectives. It's also a smart way to identify potential blind spots before they become roadblocks.

The key is diversity of ideas. Don't just bring in the usual suspects. Involve a mix of voices—different departments, levels of seniority, and lived experiences. These varied perspectives will help you craft a plan that works on paper and in practice.

Empower Managers

If leadership sets the tone, mid-level managers set the tempo. They're the ones who translate high-level goals into day-to-day realities, and they're often the first line of support for employees navigating the transition. But this role isn't easy, especially in times of upheaval.

To set managers up for success, equip them with the tools and training to lead effectively in the new structure. This might mean providing scripts for difficult conversations, hosting Q&A sessions where they can voice concerns, or offering workshops on change management and team dynamics. Managers can cascade that confidence to their teams when they feel confident and supported.

Common Pitfalls and Mistakes to Avoid When Restructuring

Even when it's well-intentioned and carefully planned, restructuring can leave people frustrated or even angry. By knowing where others often go wrong, you can sidestep those traps and lead your team through change with less turbulence (and fewer headaches).

Going Too Fast, Too Soon

Rushing a change is a common mistake. Leaders can get so caught up in the urgency of change that they plow ahead without pausing to talk to the people it will affect. Decisions are made in closed-door meetings, and before anyone knows it, new roles, reporting structures, or workflows are announced. The result? Confusion. Panic. A lot of "Why didn't anyone ask us?" vibes.

Before you roll out significant changes, slow down. Consult the people who will live with the outcomes. Ask for their input. Even if you can't incorporate every suggestion, showing that you care about their perspective can go a long way in building trust and easing transitions.

Ignoring Cultural Readiness

Not every organization is ready for change, even if it's badly needed. For example, if you walk into a new role and realize that the structure is too hierarchical and you want to open it up to allow for more collaboration, that can be challenging if people have become too used to rigid structures and unspoken power dynamics. Instead of collaboration, you might get confusion or even power struggles as people try to figure out the "new rules."

Change is about people. Prepare them first. Talk about what's coming and why it matters. And don't just focus on the logistics; address the culture shifts that will need to happen, too. Change succeeds when people are prepared to embrace it.

Failing to Communicate the 'Why'

If you've ever been on the receiving end of a restructuring, you know how frustrating it is when the "why" is a mystery. Without clear communication, your team is left to fill in the blanks. And guess what? They rarely assume the best. Cynicism grows. Rumors spread. Resistance kicks in.

Make the "why" a central part of your plan. Share the reasoning behind the changes, early and often. Be transparent about the problems you're trying to solve and the opportunities you're trying to create. And don't just stop with the "why." Explain how the changes will affect teams and individuals, and give them space to ask questions.

The One-and-Done Approach

Change isn't a one-and-done thing. It's an ongoing process. But too often, leaders treat restructuring like a big project with a neat finish line. They announce the changes, maybe hold follow-up meetings, and then move on. Meanwhile, employees are left wondering how to adapt, and the organization risks falling back into old patterns.

Restructuring doesn't end when the new org chart is published. You need to check in. Are the changes working? What's going well, and what isn't? Where do people need more support? Iterate as needed. Change is dynamic, and your approach should be, too.

Testing and Evolving

Organizations change. People grow. Priorities shift. But far too often, leaders cling to structures as if set in stone, terrified of rocking the boat. Structure isn't static. It's a living, breathing thing that needs to grow and adapt with your people and your goals.

This doesn't mean tearing everything down at the first sign of change. Instead, be open to evolution. Start small. Try piloting a new approach. Reorganize a team, tweak reporting lines, or experiment with a new workflow. Then, see what happens. Did it work? Did it solve a problem or create new ones? Ask the people living it. Be willing to listen even if the answers aren't what you hoped.

The key here is iteration. Test. Learn. Adapt. Repeat. A structure that thrived during steady growth might collapse under the weight of a crisis. A setup that fostered collaboration two years ago might feel outdated and clunky now. That's not failure. That's normal. The best leaders don't view these moments as setbacks. They see them as opportunities to improve.

Don't forget who this is all for. A responsive structure helps you hit organizational goals and streamline workflows, but it also helps the people who have to navigate that structure daily. When leaders approach change by considering how adjustments will impact employees, they create a culture where people feel valued and empowered to bring their best selves to work.

Change isn't just doing things differently. It's doing things better for the people who make it happen.

♥

Insights and Impact Plan

Hype-Free Insights

- **Structure Defines Culture**: Organizational structure shapes how people collaborate, innovate, and connect, influencing the overall culture.
- **Empathy Strengthens Connection:** Empathetic structures prioritize trust, collaboration, and support, fostering innovation and employee engagement.
- **Silos Hinder Progress:** Breaking down silos between departments creates synergy, consistent messaging, and unified missions.

- **Flexibility Enables Resilience:** Adaptable structures empower teams to pivot quickly during challenges, fostering agility without overburdening employees.
- **Growth Opportunities Drive Engagement:** Clear pathways for advancement, mentorship, and skill-building make employees feel valued and increase their loyalty and enthusiasm.
- **Balance Autonomy with Support:** Providing employees the freedom to innovate while offering resources and guidance builds trust, creativity, and productivity.
- Iteration is Key to Success: Structures must evolve alongside organizational goals and employee needs, with leaders continuously testing, learning, and adapting.

Impact Plan

- **Assess and Adjust Reporting Lines:** Identify bottlenecks, communication gaps, or unclear responsibilities in your structure, and reorganize as needed to enhance clarity and efficiency.
- **Create Cross-Functional Teams:** Form teams with diverse perspectives to tackle shared challenges, ensuring alignment across departments and fostering collaboration.
- **Foster Growth Through Career Pathways:** Develop clear career roadmaps and mentorship opportunities to guide employees toward personal and professional growth.

- **Pilot and Iterate New Structures:** Test changes like reorganized teams or workflows, gather feedback, and refine approaches to ensure structures meet current and future needs.
- **Build Flexibility into Policies:** Implement adaptable policies and systems that allow teams to respond effectively to crises or changing priorities without creating burnout.

Chapter 13
Empathy-Driven Leadership Exercises

For too long, leadership has been defined by outdated ideals. The strongest leaders, we were told, are the ones who command authority, suppress emotion, and refuse to second-guess themselves. But that model of leadership is crumbling. Today, the most effective leaders aren't those who dominate the room, but those who listen. They don't just direct; they support. They don't just speak; they understand.

Through a series of empathy-driven leadership exercises, you'll learn how to strengthen your ability to lead with care and conviction.

Empathy Mapping Exercise

Empathy mapping is a tool that can help you better understand the people you lead. You aren't guessing what they're feeling. You're building a fuller picture of their experiences and motivations. By understanding the people you lead more deeply, you can provide more meaningful support and create an environment where everyone feels valued.

Objective: The purpose of empathy mapping isn't just

to "fix" problems—it's to lead with intention. When you understand someone's experiences and challenges, you can respond in ways that build trust and motivation.

How it Works:

Step 1: Choose Your Focus: Decide whose perspective you're mapping. It could be:

- A team member struggling with a heavy workload.
- A new employee adjusting to your team's culture.

Step 2: Set Up the Map Divide a large sheet of paper, whiteboard, or digital workspace into four quadrants:

- **What they think**: What might be running through their mind? What are their fears, doubts, or goals?
- **What they feel**: What emotions might they be experiencing? Stress? Excitement? Frustration?
- **What they say**: What do they express out loud? Are there phrases or concerns they repeat?
- **What they do**: How are they behaving? What actions or patterns might reflect their internal experience?

Step 3: Fill in the Details: Bring the person or group to life by brainstorming specific insights for each quadrant:

- **What they think**: "I'm falling behind on this project," or "Will I ever catch up?"
- **What they feel**: Overwhelmed, undervalued, or motivated to prove themselves.
- **What they say**: "I need more time," or "I'm swamped right now."
- **What they do**: Work late hours, avoid asking for help, or miss deadlines.

Use feedback, observations, and data to make the map as accurate as possible. Invite others to contribute their perspectives if you're working with a team.

Step 4: Identify Patterns and Pain Points: Once your map is complete, look for recurring themes or challenges. These insights can reveal what's driving someone's behavior and where they might need more support.

Step 5: Take Action: Use your empathy map to guide your leadership or processes. For example, If a team member feels overwhelmed and thinks they're not supported, you might prioritize clearer communication about expectations or redistribute workloads.

♥

Empathy-Driven Decision Audit

Leadership means making decisions—big, small, and everything in between. But it's easy for decisions to focus too much on logistics or external pressures, overlooking the human impact. That's where an Empathy-Driven Decision Audit comes in. It's a tool to help leaders pause and intentionally factor in their choices' emotional and practical consequences.

Objective: This audit ensures your decisions are aligned with the needs and emotions of your stakeholders.

How it Works:

Step 1: Define the Decision: Start by clearly identifying the decision you're making. For example:

- Announcing a reorganization of the department.
- Sharing a change in the project management process.
- Updating policies around remote work or flexible schedules.

Be specific about what's on the table and who will be affected.

Step 2: Identify Key Audiences: List the groups most impacted by the decision. For example:

- Individual team members.
- Units within your department or division.
- The whole division.
- Other audiences on campus.

Don't lump everyone together—each group might experience the decision differently.

Step 3: Ask Empathy-Driven Questions

For each audience, ask:

- **How will this decision impact them emotionally?** Will it create excitement, relief, or pride? Or could it spark anxiety, frustration, or confusion?
- **How will this decision impact them practically?** Will it make their day-to-day lives easier or harder? Will it create new barriers or remove existing ones?
- **What challenges might this create for them?** Are there unintended consequences you hadn't considered?
- **How will we address these challenges?** Can I mitigate negative impacts or provide additional support? What's my plan for communicating the decision with empathy?

Step 4: Document Your Insights: Write down your answers. Create a transparent, thoughtful record of how people's experiences are factored into the decision.

Step 5: Use Insights to Shape the Final Decision: Your audit isn't just a formality—it's a guide. Once you've documented your findings, revisit the decision. Ask:

- Do the benefits outweigh the challenges for each audience?
- Are there tweaks we can make to minimize the negative impact?

- How can I communicate this decision with empathy and clarity?

♥

The "See Through Their Eyes" Exercise

What is the best way to understand someone's experience? See the world through their eyes. This exercise asks you to pause your perspective to explore how someone else might feel and respond to a particular scenario. By stepping into another person's shoes—even for a moment—you can uncover insights that help you communicate more effectively and make decisions that work.

Objective: This exercise helps you pause and ask, "What might this feel like for them?" It's a practice of empathy in action, and it gives you the tools to create solutions, strategies, or communications that feel thoughtful, human, and relatable.

How it Works:

Step 1: Choose a Scenario: Start with a real situation your team or organization is facing. The scenario should be specific enough to feel real but broad enough to impact multiple people. Some examples include:

- Implementing a policy change (e.g., a return-to-office mandate or updated vacation policy).
- Navigating a project delay or restructuring.
- Launching a new initiative with tight deadlines.

Step 2: Identify the Perspective: Pick a person or group affected by the scenario. Think about their role, responsibilities, and how they might uniquely experience the situation. Be as specific as possible to make their experience come to life. An example might be:

- A junior employee trying to find their footing in a reorganization.
- A working parent navigating new office attendance policies.
- A long-tenured staff member resistant to a cultural shift.

Step 3: Write From Their Point of View: Write a journal entry, letter, or inner monologue as if you were them. Imagine their day-to-day realities, their emotional state, and how they might react to the situation. Here are some prompts to guide you:

- **What's their initial reaction to this change or challenge?** (Excitement? Confusion? Frustration?)
- **What are they worried about?** (Unclear expectations? Increased workload? Job security?)
- **What do they hope for?** (More clarity? Support from leadership? A smoother transition?)
- **What might they need to feel confident or reassured?** (More communication? A chance to ask questions? Flexibility?)

For example, if you're writing as a junior employee

navigating a reorganization, your entry might sound like this:

"It's been a week since they announced the reorg, and I still don't know what this means for my role. My manager says things will be clearer soon, but every meeting feels vague. I've worked so hard to prove myself in this position, and now I'm wondering if all of that was for nothing. Will I still get the chance to lead the projects I care about? Or will I get shuffled into something less meaningful? I wish someone would give us a timeline or acknowledge how stressful this is."

Step 4: Reflect: After writing, step back and reflect on what you've captured. What emotions, challenges, or needs did you uncover? How can you apply that to your work and your leadership?

Chapter 14
Final Thoughts

As we wrap up, I hope you see that great marketing isn't just telling your institution's story—it's helping real people see themselves as part of it.

So, where do you start? It's very simple. Start small. Start with one simple question: "How do I want this person to feel when they experience our brand?" Whether it's a campus tour, a social media post, or even a phone call from admissions, that's your guiding light. Make people feel seen. Make them feel valued. Make them feel like they matter—because they do.

This work isn't easy. Empathy takes effort. It takes listening (a lot of listening). And it takes creativity. You must be willing to do things differently, stop playing it safe, and embrace the boldness of genuinely seeing people.

But the payoff is worth it. Because when you market and lead with empathy, you're building relationships. You're building connections that last long after the graduation caps are tossed. You're creating a story and a culture that people want to be part of.

So here's my challenge to you: Let go of the hype. Lean into the heart. The heart of your audience. The heart of your institution. And the heart of the work we do every day. Because when we put people first we don't just make better marketing. We make a better world.

Let's stop shouting into the void. Let's create something real.

And let's put heart over hype.

Acknowledgments

No journey is ever traveled alone, and this book is no exception. I owe immense gratitude to those who have walked alongside me on this path.

To my husband, **Dave Hunt**, my tireless champion of more than 30 years: Thank you for always being in my corner. Your unwavering belief in me and endless encouragement have been my anchor. I am forever grateful for your love and faith. I wouldn't be who I am without you. Thank you from the bottom of my heart.

To my parents, **Jim and Diane Cegla**, who instilled in me a deep belief in the transformative power of higher education: Thank you for paving the way for my dreams. You ensured I had the opportunity to attend college, and in doing so, you opened the door to a life I once only imagined. Your sacrifices and support have shaped me into who I am today.

To my sisters, **Michelle Rakos** and **Teresa Cegla,** and their partners **Dale Jansen** and **C.J. Reindl**: Thank you for cheering me on through the grueling process of writing this book. I love you more.

To the leaders who mentored me in my early career and created spaces of psychological safety, **John Healy, Richard Wells, Danny Kemp**, and **Elwood Robinson**: You gave me the freedom to grow, lead, and embrace my full potential. Thank you for seeing something in me and allowing me to become the leader I was meant to be. Your trust and belief in my abilities have been transformative gifts.

To **Amber Kennedy**, who helped me push my book in this direction: Thank you for inspiring me to take the content I'd been working on for years and turn it into something tangible.

To **Christy Jackson**: You may be the president of my fan club, but I am the president of yours. Thank you for every word of encouragement you have ever given me over the last fifteen years.

To **Jamie Ceman**: Despite the egregious way you spell your name, your friendship has been such a valuable part of my higher ed journey. We've been there for each other's ups and downs and I'll always appreciate that.

To **Amitoj Kaur**, my accountability partner through this journey: You have no idea how truly remarkable you are. Thank you for your friendship and support. I can't wait to read your book!

To **Bart Caylor**, who pushed me to write this book back in 2023 and gave me invaluable insights into the process along the way. You've always been a great cheerleader and I appreciate it so much!

To **Day Kibilds** and **Ashley Budd**: Thank you for all the advice you gave me as I worked on this book. You helped me get out of my head and push through every time I thought, "I can't do this."

To early readers **Nate Jorgensen, Christian Ponce, Devin Purgason**, **Jessica Rivinius**, and **Elwood Robinson**: Thank you for the time you took to read the entire book and offer feedback.

To **Alex Hammond**, editor extraordinaire: Thank you

for your insightful feedback and for cleaning up my grammar and catching my typos.

Finally, to **everyone who has supported me throughout my career**, whether through kind words, collaboration, or simply showing up: Your encouragement and belief in me have carried me further than I ever thought possible. I am grateful beyond measure for every conversation, shared vision, and moment of connection that has enriched this journey.

This book is a reflection of all of you. Thank you for being a part of my story.

About the Author

Photo by Dave Hunt

Jaime Hunt is the founder and president of Solve Higher Ed Marketing, a consulting firm she launched in 2024 after a 20-year career in higher education—including nearly a decade as a chief marketing officer. A storyteller at heart, she specializes in branding, marketing, empathetic leadership, and cutting through the noise to create meaningful connections.

Jaime began her career as a print journalist before transitioning to higher education in 2004. Over the years, she has led efforts in media relations, marketing, branding, digital communications, crisis communications, and enrollment marketing. Her leadership roles include serving as vice president and chief communications and marketing officer at Old Dominion University, Miami University (Ohio), and Winston-Salem State University. Earlier in her career, she held marketing and communications positions at Radford University, the University of Wisconsin Oshkosh, and Northwestern Health Sciences University.

A passionate educator and keynote speaker, Jaime also teaches graduate courses in higher education marketing and emerging media at West Virginia University. She has taken the stage at conferences around the world, earned more than 40 industry awards, and served as a dedicated volunteer with organizations like the American Marketing Association, the Public Relations Society of America, and the Council for the Advancement and Support of Higher Education.

Jaime holds a bachelor's degree in journalism from the University of Minnesota and a master's in integrated marketing communications from West Virginia University. She is also a graduate of the Arizona State University/Georgetown University Academy for Innovative Higher Education Leadership.

She lives in coastal Virginia, where she shares her home with her husband, Dave, an elderly dog named Maeby, and a surprisingly social tortoise, ClemBob. When she's not helping institutions elevate their brands, you can probably find her on the water—happiest with the wind in her hair and a boat beneath her feet.

To learn more about Jaime or to inquire about having

her speak at your event, visit SolveHigherEd.com or Heart OverHypeBook.com or follow her on LinkedIn at LinkedIn.com/in/jaimehunt.